Baking with Agave Nectar

Baking with Agave Nectar

Over 100 Recipes Using Nature's Ultimate Sweetener

ANIA CATALANO

PHOTOGRAPHS BY LARA HATA

CELESTIAL ARTS
Berkeley

THIS BOOK IS DEDICATED TO THE TWO LOVES OF MY LIFE—MY HUSBAND,
JOE, AND OUR DAUGHTER, SOFIA (OUR LITTLE MIRACLE).

Copyright © 2008 by Ania Catalano
Photography © 2008 by Lara Hata

All rights reserved. Published in the United States by
Celestial Arts, an imprint of the Crown Publishing Group,
a division of Random House, Inc., New York.
www.crownpublishing.com
www.tenspeed.com

Celestial Arts and the Celestial Arts colophon are registered
trademarks of Random House, Inc

Library of Congress Cataloging-in-Publication Data
on file with publisher

ISBN-13: 978-1-58761-321-0

Printed in China

Cover and text design by Robin Terra | terra studio
Food and prop styling by George Dolese
Photography assistant: Ha Huynh
Food stylist assistant: Elizabet de Nederlanden

12 11 10 9 8 7 6 5 4

First Edition

Contents

Introduction

MY INTRODUCTION TO NATURAL FOODS TOOK PLACE ABOUT
twenty years ago when I was diagnosed with hypoglycemia. At the
time, it felt like I had two jobs—working full-time as an interior
designer and working the rest of the time trying to figure out what,
when, and how to eat in order to feel healthy. I always enjoyed good
food, frequented gourmet restaurants, traveled, and loved to cook, yet
suddenly I was forced to make a change in my diet in order to improve
my health, especially since diabetes was prevalent in my family. I began
to explore the world of whole foods, experimenting with them and
using them to replace the refined foods in my diet.

Needless to say, it changed my life. I began to feel great, had endless
energy, and finally felt satisfied when I ate, all due to replacing refined
ingredients with whole, natural foods. So great was my newfound
passion that I became a whole foods chef, first enrolling in the Natural
Gourmet School of Cooking in New York, and then opening Sprouts
Natural Foods Market & Café in Trumbull, Connecticut, in 1989.

Being totally immersed in the natural foods business and having
hypoglycemia, I was always on the lookout for new and improved
sweeteners to use in preparing desserts and other baked goods. In the
mid-1990s, I discovered agave nectar. Of all the sweeteners I had ever
used—Sucanat, brown rice syrup, barley malt, honey, maple syrup,
date sugar, fruit concentrates, and stevia—agave nectar was the only
sweetener that had no shortcomings. While some sweeteners were
great tasting, they were off limits to me because they were refined and
spiked my blood sugar levels. Other sugar alternatives were better
from a health perspective (i.e., lower glycemic index), but either the
taste or texture when prepared in foods was lacking. And then came
agave. It was low-glycemic, delicious, easy to use, and best of all I felt
great after eating it. I did not experience the symptoms of sugar rush,
like palpitations, that would invariably occur after I had consumed

high-glycemic sweeteners. Many of my customers with diabetes and other health issues agreed. For me, the search for the ultimate natural sweetener was over.

What Is Agave Nectar?

Agave nectar is a natural, organic, Kosher, plant-based sweetener made from several varieties of the agave plant—primarily the 'Blue Weber' variety, which is the same one used to make tequila. Agave grows wild in Jalisco State in Mexico, and while Indians there discovered the plant's many uses thousands of years ago, agave nectar was not widely marketed until the 1990s.

The agave plant must be 7 to 10 years old before its sugars are at their peak and ready for harvesting. A mature plant can stand 5 to 8 feet tall and have a diameter of 7 to 12 feet! The plant is cut free from its roots and the spiky leaves are removed, leaving behind the *piña* (so called because it resembles a huge pineapple). The *piña* is capped with a stone and a milky juice collects in the center. Harvesters ladle out the juice, which is cleaned and filtered to create the liquid that will become the agave nectar. A gentle enzymatic process breaks down the carbohydrates into sugars, resulting in a complex form of fructose called inulinar fructose. No processing chemicals are ever used in agave nectar production, making it a completely safe, unrefined, and organic sweetener for children and adults alike.

The Sweet Science of Agave Nectar

Agave nectars are low-glycemic sweeteners, due to their high fructose to glucose ratio. What does this mean? Certain carbohydrates (like refined flour, white rice, white potatoes, and of course, refined sugar) cause blood sugar (glucose) and insulin levels to spike and crash. The glycemic index (GI) ranks foods according to how quickly they are processed into glucose in the body. Pure glucose, with a GI of 100, is the reference point: the lower the GI, the more slowly the food is processed and the less dramatic the fluctuations in blood glucose and insulin levels. Health experts agree that controlling these levels is an important component in lowering risk for heart disease and diabetes, reducing cholesterol levels, and managing weight.

Keeping your blood sugar levels in check by eating lower-GI foods that are fiber-rich, such as whole grains, whole grain flours, vegetables, and fruits in combination with the proper sweeteners can also help you feel full and satisfied longer after meals, therefore aiding in weight loss.

While the GI of agave nectar varies from one manufacturer to another, all are considered low-glycemic if their GI is 55 or below. Premium 'Blue Weber' agave has been found to produce the best tasting sweetener, as well as one with the lowest glycemic index, generally in the range of 19 to 39. Compare this to honey (GI of 35 to 64), pure maple syrup (GI of about 54), and table sugar (GI of 60 to 65). Various glycemic index testing centers around the world have studied agave nectar extensively, and the consensus is that this sweetener is safe and suitable for most diabetics and others monitoring their blood sugar levels. Agave nectar has met the food exchange requirements set by the American Diabetic Association for product labeling. As with any sweetener, agave nectar should be used in moderation and with discretion by people under medical supervision. People with diabetes or other metabolic disorders should consult with their doctor to determine how this product will fit into their personal health management program.

Using Agave Nectar

Agave nectar is a little less viscous than honey, and it has a stable three-year shelf life. It does not crystallize or solidify when cold, pouring and dissolving easily even in cold liquids. Because it has excellent moisture retaining properties, it is ideal for creating breads and baked goods with light and fluffy texture; it also works to keep them fresher for a longer period of time.

Agave nectar can be used straight out of the bottle to sweeten teas, coffee, lemonade, and other beverages, and it's a delicious topping for pancakes, waffles, or your morning breakfast cereal. And wow, does it make an awesome margarita! (More on that later in the book.)

Agave nectars are sold in light, amber, dark, and raw varieties. Light agave nectar has a mild, almost neutral flavor, and is a great choice for use in delicate tasting desserts, baked goods, sauces, and beverages. Amber agave nectar has a medium-intensity caramel flavor, and is suitable for many desserts, as well as sauces and savory dishes. It is an excellent "straight out of the bottle" syrup. Dark agave nectar has stronger caramel notes, and imparts a delicious and distinct flavor to many desserts. It's best used in poultry, meat, and seafood dishes, and is wonderful as a topping for pancakes and waffles. Raw agave nectar also has a mild, neutral taste. It is produced at temperatures below 118°F to protect the natural enzymes, so this variety is a perfect sweetener for raw foodists and the health conscious. In the recipes in this book, I often recommend a specific variety, but feel free to use whichever variety pleases you best.

When adapting a recipe to use agave nectar, reduce the other liquids by one-third. When replacing table sugar, plan on using about 25 percent less agave nectar to achieve the same level of sweetness; for example, use $^3/_4$ cup of agave nectar for every cup of sugar. Use it 1:1 to replace honey in recipes. Also, baked goods with agave nectar brown more quickly, so reduce oven temperatures by 25°F to avoid burning.

Since fructose is sweeter than sucrose, less agave nectar is needed to achieve the same level of sweetness as table sugar. Agave nectar has only 45 calories and 11 grams of carbohydrates per tablespoon. Since you need less to sweeten the same as sugar, you will also be cutting back on calories. It's a wonderful way to help you and your family break the sugar habit.

Becoming a mom definitely solidified my thoughts on the importance of healthy eating. Like all parents, I want what's best for my daughter. I know that by helping her develop healthy eating habits I am preparing her to make good choices in the future. That's why you'll find lots of kid-friendly desserts and snacks in this book to get you started. I've developed desserts that are appropriate for adults and kids with dietary restrictions and allergies, so some of the recipes are vegan and some are gluten-free. I've noted them as such.

I am a dessert lover and whole-foods chef who began baking to provide delicious, whole-grain, sugar-free goodies for myself and my customers. So the recipes in this book are realistic. Some of them can be whipped up in minutes but look like you've been slaving in the kitchen all day. That's my kind of dessert!

I invite you to try these agave nectar recipes created with passion and a love of sharing delicious, healthy food with friends and family. I hope you enjoy trying them as much as I did creating them. And I hope they inspire you to create a few masterpieces of your own.

Muffins, Tea Breads, and Breakfast Dishes

Spicy Pumpkin Muffins

MAKES | 12 MUFFINS

These muffins are another way to add fiber and nutrient-rich veggies to your day. Pack a little more nutritional punch into this recipe by using organic canned pumpkin.

1 cup oat flour

1 cup barley flour

2 teaspoons baking powder

½ teaspoon sea salt

1 teaspoon ground cinnamon

½ teaspoon ground nutmeg

¼ teaspoon ground cloves

¼ teaspoon ground allspice

½ cup low-fat milk or unsweetened soy milk

1 large egg, lightly beaten

½ cup amber agave nectar

¼ cup canola oil

2 teaspoons vanilla extract

2 cups canned organic pumpkin or
   puréed fresh pumpkin

½ cup raisins

⅓ cup walnuts, coarsely chopped

¼ cup raw pumpkin seeds

Preheat the oven to 350°F. Line 12 muffin cups with paper liners.

Mix together the oat flour, barley flour, baking powder, salt, cinnamon, nutmeg, cloves, and allspice in a large bowl. In another bowl, mix the milk, egg, agave nectar, canola oil, vanilla extract, and pumpkin. Pour the milk mixture over the dry ingredients and mix until just combined. Fold in the raisins, walnuts, and pumpkin seeds. Spoon the batter into the prepared muffin cups and bake for 25 minutes, or until a toothpick inserted into the center of a muffin comes out clean.

Cranberry Orange Muffins

MAKES | 12 MUFFINS

Cranberry and orange is a classic, tangy flavor combination. Stock up and freeze fresh cranberries when in season for baking throughout the year. For a sweet and chewy alternative, try fruit-sweetened dried cranberries, which are similar to raisins.

2 large eggs, or 4 large egg whites
  or ½ cup egg substitute
½ cup light agave nectar
¼ cup canola oil
¼ cup unsweetened applesauce
1 cup nonfat plain yogurt
Juice plus freshly grated zest of 1 orange
½ cup wheat bran
2 cups sprouted whole wheat flour
  or sprouted spelt flour
1 tablespoon baking powder
½ teaspoon baking soda
½ teaspoon salt
½ teaspoon ground cinnamon
¼ teaspoon ground nutmeg
1½ cups fresh or frozen cranberries, chopped

Preheat the oven to 375°F. Line 12 muffin cups with paper liners.

Combine the eggs, agave nectar, canola oil, applesauce, yogurt, orange juice, orange zest, and wheat bran in a large bowl. In a separate bowl, combine the flour, baking powder, baking soda, salt, cinnamon, and nutmeg. Mix the wet and dry ingredients together gently. Fold in the cranberries. Spoon the batter into the prepared muffin cups and bake for 20 minutes, or until a toothpick inserted into the center of a muffin comes out clean.

Orange Pecan Granola

MAKES | 10 CUPS   ✺ VEGAN

I first made this delicious, super-crunchy granola while consulting for Edge of the Woods, a great natural foods market, bakery, and vegetarian café in New Haven, Connecticut. At the time, I was developing lots of agave nectar desserts and goodies for diabetics and clients concerned with sugar when it occurred to me that there were no good-tasting, sugar-free granolas available. Hence the birth of Orange Pecan Granola, a staple in our household! Great on its own as a snack, or sprinkle it over yogurt, fresh fruit, or even frozen yogurt for dessert.

6 cups regular rolled oats
  (not quick cooking)
1 cup oat bran
1 cup ground flax meal
1 cup almond meal (ground raw almonds)
¼ cup sesame seeds
1¾ cups unsweetened applesauce
1 cup light agave nectar (or 1⅓ cups
  for sweeter granola)
1 tablespoon vanilla extract
1 tablespoon orange extract
2½ tablespoons cinnamon
½ teaspoon cloves
1 teaspoon nutmeg, freshly grated
½ teaspoon sea salt
¼ cup canola oil
1 cup currants or raisins
1½ cups pecans, coarsely chopped
  (try other nuts for variety)

Preheat oven to 300°F.

Combine all ingredients except pecans and mix well. Add pecans and mix again. Spread mixture evenly on a lightly greased cookie sheet. Bake until slightly golden—about 1 hour, stirring occasionally. Remove from oven, stir in currants, and let cool. Stored in an airtight container the granola should keep for approximately 2 months.

Zucchini Date Muffins

MAKES | 12 MUFFINS

I keep a batch of these low-fat muffins in my freezer at all times. They stand in as cupcakes when my daughter, Sofia, asks, "What's for dessert?" For a quick and easy low-fat frosting, spread a little Greek-style yogurt over the top, drizzle with agave nectar, and add a sprinkle of cinnamon. Perfect!

3 cups sprouted spelt flour
   or sprouted whole wheat flour
3 tablespoons ground flaxseeds
2 teaspoons baking powder
1 teaspoon baking soda
½ teaspoon salt
1 teaspoon ground cinnamon
½ teaspoon ground nutmeg
1 large egg, or 2 large egg whites
   or ¼ cup egg substitute
¾ cup light agave nectar
¼ cup canola oil
¾ cup water
¼ cup nonfat plain yogurt
2 teaspoons vanilla extract
Freshly grated zest of 1 orange
2 cups grated zucchini, including skin
   (about 2 medium zucchini)
¾ cup pitted dates, chopped

Preheat the oven to 350°F. Line 12 muffin cups with paper liners.

In a bowl, combine the flour, flaxseeds, baking powder, baking soda, salt, cinnamon, and nutmeg. In a separate bowl, mix together the egg, agave nectar, canola oil, water, yogurt, vanilla extract, and orange zest. Mix together the wet and dry ingredients until just combined. Fold in the zucchini and dates. Spoon the batter into the prepared muffin cups and bake for 20 minutes, or until a toothpick inserted into the center of a muffin comes out clean.

Sunrise Carrot Muffins

MAKES | 12 MUFFINS ☀ VEGAN

These muffins are loaded with good-for-you veggies, fruits, and seeds—and they're vegan, too. The silken tofu replaces the dairy and eggs, and adds moistness and protein for a tasty breakfast or afternoon snack.

2 cups sprouted spelt flour or
    sprouted whole wheat flour
1 tablespoon baking powder
1½ teaspoons ground cinnamon
½ teaspoon ground nutmeg
¼ teaspoon ground cloves
¼ cup flaxseeds
1 cup raisins
12 ounces firm silken tofu
¼ cup canola oil
⅔ cup light agave nectar
1 teaspoon vanilla extract
1 cup grated carrots (about 4 medium carrots)
1 apple, peeled, cored, and chopped
¼ cup raw pumpkin seeds

Preheat the oven to 350°F. Line 12 muffin cups with paper liners.

Sift together the flour, baking powder, cinnamon, nutmeg, and cloves. Mix in the flaxseeds and raisins. Place tofu, canola oil, agave nectar, and vanilla extract in a food processor and blend until smooth and creamy, about 1 to 2 minutes. Add the tofu mixture to the flour mixture and combine well. Fold in the carrots, apple, and pumpkin seeds. Spoon the batter into the prepared muffin cups and bake for 15 to 20 minutes, until a toothpick inserted into the center of a muffin comes out clean.

Quinoa Corn Blueberry Muffins

MAKES | 12 MUFFINS

These are some of my favorite muffins. The quinoa flour and cornmeal give them a beautiful golden color and a nice texture, a perfect combination with the juicy blueberries.

1 cup cornmeal
1 cup quinoa flour
3 teaspoons baking powder
1½ teaspoons baking soda
½ teaspoon sea salt
1 large egg, beaten
⅓ cup light agave nectar
¼ cup canola oil
1 teaspoon vanilla extract
1 cup nonfat plain yogurt
Freshly grated zest of 1 lemon
1½ cups fresh or frozen blueberries

Preheat the oven to 350°F. Line 12 muffin cups with paper liners.

In a bowl, mix together the cornmeal, quinoa flour, baking powder, baking soda, and salt. In a separate bowl, mix together the egg, agave nectar, canola oil, vanilla extract, yogurt, and lemon zest. Pour the egg mixture into the bowl with the dry ingredients and stir until incorporated. Gently stir in the blueberries. Spoon the batter into the prepared muffin cups and bake for 25 minutes, or until a toothpick inserted into the center of a muffin comes out clean.

Power Bran Muffins

MAKES | 12 MUFFINS

Chock full of whole grains, flaxseeds, and dried fruit, these delicious muffins are a tasty way to add fiber to your diet. Soaking the raisins and bran in the liquid ingredients helps keep the muffins moist.

1 cup raisins or fruit juice–sweetened dried blueberries, chopped if large

1 cup wheat bran

1 cup soy milk, or ½ cup nonfat plain yogurt mixed with ½ cup water

½ cup amber agave nectar

¼ cup canola oil

2 large eggs, beaten, or 4 large egg whites or ½ cup egg substitute

1 cup sprouted whole wheat flour or sprouted spelt flour

½ cup wheat germ

¼ cup ground flaxseeds

1 teaspoon baking powder

½ teaspoon baking soda

1 teaspoon ground cinnamon

Pinch of sea salt

Preheat the oven to 375°F. Line 12 muffin cups with paper liners.

In a bowl, combine the raisins, wheat bran, soy milk, agave nectar, canola oil, and eggs and let sit for 10 minutes. In a another bowl, combine the flour, wheat germ, flaxseeds, baking powder, baking soda, cinnamon, and salt. Combine the two mixtures until incorporated. Spoon the batter into the prepared muffin cups and bake for 20 minutes, or until a toothpick inserted into the center of a muffin comes out clean.

Stuffed French Toast with Caramelized Cinnamon Apples

SERVES | 4

My client and friend Jeff Valko, whose personal chef I've been for years, loves this French toast. Being health-conscious and an exercise nut (like me), he likes to start his day with a protein boost. The apple topping is also delicious served over ice cream or frozen yogurt.

FILLING

1⅓ cups low-fat whipped cottage cheese
   or low-fat ricotta cheese
3 tablespoons light agave nectar
½ teaspoon ground cinnamon
1 teaspoon freshly grated lemon zest
⅓ cup raisins (optional)

FRENCH TOAST

8 slices regular or cinnamon raisin
   sprouted grain bread
2 large eggs plus 1 large egg white,
   beaten, 5 large egg whites, or
   ⅔ cup egg substitute
2 cups 1 percent low-fat milk
   or unsweetened soy milk
2 scoops sugar-free vanilla whey
   protein powder
1 teaspoon vanilla extract
Pinch of sea salt
¼ cup light agave nectar

APPLES

2 tablespoons unsalted butter or
   nonhydrogenated butter substitute
3 Granny Smith apples, peeled, cored, and sliced
1 teaspoon ground cinnamon
½ cup light agave nectar

Lightly oil a baking sheet and set aside. Spray a large nonstick skillet with canola oil spray. Preheat the oven to 350°F.

To make the filling, mix together all the ingredients in a bowl.

To make the French toast, lay out four slices of bread on a clean work surface and spread evenly with the filling mixture. Place the remaining slices of bread on top, sandwich-style. Cut each "sandwich" on the diagonal and set aside. Whisk together the eggs, milk, whey, vanilla extract, salt, and agave nectar. Soak the sandwich halves in the egg mixture, turning them over until both sides are very moist. In the prepared skillet, sauté the sandwiches over medium heat. Brown 1 side, then carefully turn to brown the other side. Remove from the pan and place on the prepared baking sheet. Bake for 15 minutes, or until cooked through and hot on the inside.

To prepare the apple topping, melt the butter in a large sauté pan, add apples, and sauté over medium heat until softened, about 5 minutes, stirring often. Add the cinnamon and agave nectar and cook together for a few minutes more until the mixture is bubbly and the apples are tender. Spoon the mixture over the French toast.

Whole Wheat Crêpes with Strawberries and Cream

SERVES | 6 ✺ VEGAN

The filling for these crêpes is made with mirin, a Japanese cooking wine made from sweet brown rice. You can find it at health food stores, Asian food stores, and possibly your local supermarket. This is a fabulous vegan dish, ideal for brunch.

CRÊPE BATTER

2½ cups unsweetened soy milk
6 ounces firm silken tofu
2 teaspoons vanilla extract
½ teaspoon sea salt
2 teaspoons baking powder
1 tablespoon light agave nectar
2 cups whole wheat pastry flour
   or sprouted spelt flour

FILLING

1 pound regular firm tofu, drained
2 teaspoons grated orange rind
⅓ cup light agave nectar
⅛ teaspoon sea salt
¼ cup mirin
1 teaspoon vanilla extract

TOPPING

1 pint fresh sliced strawberries

To prepare the crêpe batter, in a blender or food processor add the soy milk, tofu, vanilla extract, salt, baking powder, and agave nectar. Blend at high speed until smooth and creamy, about 1 to 2 minutes. Place the flour in a bowl, pour the liquid mixture over it, and beat to combine.

Prepare the filling by blending all the ingredients together in a food processor until smooth and creamy, about 2 to 3 minutes.

To cook the crêpes, heat a small oiled skillet or crêpe pan until hot. Pour in slightly less than ¼ cup of the crêpe batter. Tilt and rotate the pan to distribute the batter evenly over the bottom. Cook the crêpe until lightly flecked with brown (lift the crêpe by the edge to check). Turn the crêpe over and cook briefly (a few seconds) on the other side. Repeat this process, making 5 or more crêpes with the remaining batter, oiling the skillet as necessary to prevent sticking. Stack crêpes on a plate and cover with foil to keep warm.

To serve the crêpes, spoon 2 to 3 table-spoons of the filling mixture onto the middle of each crêpe, fold 1 side over the filling, then the other side, letter-style, and garnish with strawberries.

Whole Wheat Cinnamon Sticky Buns

MAKES | 1½ DOZEN   ✿ VEGAN

These cinnamon buns are well worth the extra effort to make. They're so moist, sticky, cinnamon-y, and delicious you'll never miss those sugar-laden ones sold at malls. P.S. These smell even better than "those" when they're baking . . . and they don't have a million calories. Make them vegan by using butter and milk substitutes.

FILLING

¼ cup unsalted butter or nonhydrogenated butter substitute

1 cup amber agave nectar

2 tablespoons ground cinnamon

3 tablespoons sprouted whole wheat flour or whole wheat pastry flour

1 cup walnuts, lightly toasted and finely ground in a food processor

¾ cup raisins, soaked in 1 cup boiling water for 10 minutes and drained well

DOUGH

1 large baking potato, peeled

1 tablespoon active dry yeast

½ cup warm water

¼ cup plus 2 tablespoons light agave nectar

½ cup 1 percent low-fat milk or unsweetened soy milk

3 tablespoons unsalted butter or nonhydrogenated butter substitute, melted

1 teaspoon sea salt

4 to 5 cups sprouted whole wheat flour or whole wheat pastry flour

Extra melted butter or butter substitute, for brushing

GLAZE

2 tablespoons unsalted butter or nonhydrogenated butter substitute, at room temperature

2½ tablespoons unsweetened apple juice

½ cup nonfat dry milk or unsweetened soy milk powder

½ cup light agave nectar

½ teaspoon vanilla extract

⅛ teaspoon almond extract

To make the filling, in a large bowl, using an electric mixer, cream the butter with the agave nectar until smooth, about 2 minutes. Add the cinnamon and flour and mix well. Stir in the walnuts and raisins. Refrigerate to firm the mixture for a minimum of 2 hours.

Begin the dough by cooking the potato in boiling water for 25 to 30 minutes, until soft. Drain, reserving ¾ cup of the starchy water. Mash the potato and reserved water until smooth. Set aside and cool to room temperature.

Place the yeast, warm water, and 2 tablespoons of the agave nectar in a food processor. Pulse a few times to dissolve the yeast. Let this mixture sit about 10 minutes, or until foamy. Add the cooled mashed potato, milk, the remaining ¼ cup agave nectar, the melted butter, and salt. Pulse several >

times to mix. Add the flour a little at a time, pulsing to blend until a soft dough forms. Transfer the dough to a lightly floured surface. Gently knead by hand for approximately 1 minute, or until smooth and elastic. Place the kneaded dough into a lightly oiled bowl. Let rest for 20 minutes. Punch down the dough and turn in the bowl to coat with oil. Cover the bowl with plastic wrap and place in a draft-free area to rise. Let the dough rise until doubled in bulk, about 1 hour.

While the dough is rising, prepare the glaze. Place all the glaze ingredients in a food processor and blend until smooth, about 1 minute. Refrigerate until ready to use. The mixture will thicken slightly when chilled.

To prepare the sticky buns, line 2 rectangular jelly roll pans with parchment paper and lightly spray with canola oil spray. Gently punch the dough down. Roll out on a lightly floured work surface to form an 18- by 20-inch rectangle. (The dough will be sticky to work with.) Spread the filling mixture over the dough, leaving a 1-inch border on all sides. Beginning from a long side, carefully roll the dough up to form a long log. Slice the log into 18 equal pieces. Place the slices onto the prepared pans with the edges of the rolls lightly touching together. Fill 1 pan entirely before starting the next, so most rolls will fit snuggly together. Brush the tops with the melted butter. Cover with a damp kitchen cloth and place in a warm, draft-free area. Allow the rolls to rise for 40 to 45 minutes, until doubled in size.

Preheat the oven to 375°F.

When the rolls are fully risen, bake for 25 minutes, or until lightly golden. Let the rolls cool on the pans for 10 to 15 minutes before drizzling with the glaze. Pull apart gently to serve. Best served warm.

Store the leftover rolls in the refrigerator and reheat in a 350°F oven for 10 minutes before serving.

Wild Rice, Walnut, and Cranberry Tea Bread

MAKES | 1 LOAF

This tea bread gets its nutty flavor and texture from wild rice. The nuts and cranberries inside make an appealing visual presentation. Spread a little nonfat Greek-style yogurt on top, instead of cream cheese, for a delicious low-fat breakfast.

1½ cups cooked wild rice
1 large egg, beaten
¼ cup light agave nectar
1 teaspoon vanilla extract
2 tablespoons canola oil
Freshly grated zest of 1 small orange
1¼ cups sprouted spelt flour
2 teaspoons baking powder
½ teaspoon salt
½ cup juice-sweetened dried cranberries
¾ cup walnuts, chopped

Preheat the oven to 325°F.

Lightly oil a 4- by 8-inch loaf pan and set aside. Mix together the cooked rice, egg, agave nectar, vanilla extract, canola oil, and orange zest. In a separate bowl, mix the flour, baking powder, and salt. Combine the wet and dry mixtures, then fold in the cranberries and walnuts. Pour the batter into the prepared loaf pan. Bake for 1 hour, or until a toothpick inserted into the center of the loaf comes out clean. Let cool in the pan for 5 minutes, then turn out onto a rack to cool completely. Store in the refrigerator, tightly wrapped.

Banana Date Bread

MAKES | 1 LOAF ☀ VEGAN

This is the best vegan banana bread ever—super moist and deliciously sweet from the dates.

12 ounces firm silken tofu
½ cup light agave nectar
1 cup mashed ripe bananas
¼ cup unsweetened apple juice
2 teaspoons vanilla extract
1 teaspoon ground cinnamon
½ teaspoon ground nutmeg
¼ cup canola oil
1¾ cups sprouted spelt flour or
    sprouted whole wheat flour
1 tablespoon baking powder
1 cup pitted dates, chopped
½ cup walnuts, chopped
2 tablespoons flaxseeds (optional)

Preheat the oven to 325°F.

Coat a 4- by 8-inch loaf pan with nonstick canola oil spray and flour lightly. In a food processor, combine the tofu, agave nectar, bananas, apple juice, vanilla extract, cinnamon, nutmeg, and canola oil. Blend until smooth and creamy, about 2 to 3 minutes. Sift together the flour and baking powder into a large bowl. Add the tofu mixture and mix with a wooden spoon until just blended. Fold in the dates, walnuts, and flaxseeds. Turn the batter into the prepared pan and bake for 35 to 40 minutes, until a toothpick inserted into the center of the loaf comes out clean. Let cool in the pan for 10 to 15 minutes before transferring to a rack to cool completely. Store in the refrigerator, tightly wrapped.

Cookies and Bars

Old-Fashioned Oatmeal Raisin Cookies

MAKES | 1½ DOZEN COOKIES

These cookies are moist and chewy, just like they should be. They're also secretly boosted with fiber from flaxseed meal. You don't have to tell the kids.

½ cup unsalted butter or
   nonhydrogenated butter substitute
¾ cup light agave nectar
2 large eggs
1 teaspoon vanilla extract
1½ cups sprouted spelt flour or
   whole wheat pastry flour
1¾ cups regular rolled oats
   (not quick cooking)
¼ cup golden flaxseed meal
1 teaspoon ground cinnamon
½ teaspoon baking soda
½ teaspoon sea salt
¾ cup raisins

Preheat the oven to 325°F. Line 2 baking sheets with parchment paper.

Using an electric mixer, in a large bowl cream the butter with the agave nectar until light and fluffy, about 1 to 2 minutes. Add the eggs 1 at a time and stir in the vanilla extract. In a separate bowl, combine the flour, oats, flaxseed meal, cinnamon, baking soda, and salt. Add to the butter mixture and stir until just combined. Fold in the raisins. Drop the batter by heaping tablespoonfuls onto the prepared baking sheets. Using the back of a spoon, flatten slightly and bake for 12 minutes, or until slightly browned.

Holiday Gingerbread Cookies

MAKES | 5 DOZEN COOKIES

✿ VEGAN   ✿ GLUTEN-FREE

This is a great cookie for children with gluten sensitivity. Using my daughter, her friends, and her baby-sitters as my most critical testers proved these cookies will definitely be a holiday tradition at my house. The best thing is, you can freeze part of the dough, unbaked, for later use. Just defrost in the refrigerator, roll out, and bake according to the directions for a wonderful spicy-sweet treat any time of year. If the kids, and maybe the adults, are clamoring for gingerbread people, you can add eyes, nose, and buttons by pressing raisins or currants gently into the dough before baking.

2⅓ cups brown rice flour
1½ cups amaranth flour
1½ cups arrowroot powder,
    plus extra for dusting
2 tablespoons baking powder
2 teaspoons baking soda
1 tablespoon ground cinnamon
1 teaspoon ground ginger
½ teaspoon ground nutmeg
½ teaspoon ground cloves
1 teaspoon sea salt
1 cup amber agave nectar
¼ cup dark molasses
¼ cup unsweetened applesauce
⅓ cup canola oil
2 tablespoons vanilla extract

Preheat the oven to 350°F. Line 2 baking sheets with parchment paper.

In a large bowl, stir together the rice flour, amaranth flour, arrowroot powder, baking powder, baking soda, cinnamon, ginger, nutmeg, cloves, and salt. In a separate bowl, combine the agave nectar, molasses, applesauce, canola oil, and vanilla extract. Mix well and pour over the dry ingredients. Stir until the 2 mixtures are thoroughly combined. Cover and chill the dough 2 hours or more.

Sprinkle your work surface with arrowroot powder. Divide the chilled dough into 4 equal parts. Return 3 parts to the refrigerator to keep chilled. Roll out the dough ¼ inch thick. Cut out gingerbread with cookie cutters and place them on the prepared baking sheets. Bake for 6 to 7 minutes. The cookies will be slightly soft when they are removed from the oven. Allow to cool for 5 to 10 minutes, then move to cooling racks to cool completely. These freeze very well in plastic freezer storage bags. Makes approximately 5 dozen cookies, depending on the size of the cookie cutter.

Chunky Cherry Almond Chip Cookies

MAKES | 1½ DOZEN COOKIES   VEGAN

Carob chips are a nice change from chocolate in these yummy cookies.

1 cup sprouted spelt flour
   or whole wheat pastry flour
½ cup arrowroot powder
1 teaspoon baking powder
½ teaspoon sea salt
½ teaspoon ground cinnamon
6 tablespoons canola oil
1 teaspoon vanilla extract
½ teaspoon almond extract
Freshly grated zest of ½ orange
½ cup light agave nectar
½ cup almonds, lightly toasted
   and coarsely chopped
½ cup juice-sweetened dried cherries
½ cup grain-sweetened carob chips
   or grain-sweetened chocolate chips

Preheat the oven to 350°F. Line two baking sheets with parchment paper.

In a bowl, combine the flour, arrowroot powder, baking powder, salt, and cinnamon. In another bowl, whisk together the canola oil, vanilla extract, almond extract, orange zest, and agave nectar. Combine the two mixtures until thoroughly incorporated. Fold in the almonds, cherries, and carob chips. Drop by heaping teaspoonfuls onto the prepared baking sheets. Bake about 12 minutes, or until lightly golden. Allow the cookies to cool on the sheet for 5 minutes before transferring them to cooling racks to cool completely.

Raspberry Linzer
Torte Cookies

MAKES | 3½ DOZEN COOKIES ☀ VEGAN

I've been making these irresistible cookies since opening my first Sprouts Café in Trumbull, Connecticut, years ago. I now make them with agave nectar and sprouted spelt flour, and they're better than ever.

2 cups raw almonds

2 cups regular rolled oats (not quick cooking)

2 cups sprouted spelt flour or whole wheat pastry flour

1 teaspoon ground cinnamon

⅓ cup light agave nectar

1 cup canola oil

1 cup juice-sweetened raspberry preserves or another flavor of your choice

Preheat the oven to 350°F. Line 2 baking sheets with parchment paper.

Place the almonds in a food processor and grind to a fine meal, about 1 minute. Remove and set aside. Place the oats in the food processor and grind to a fine meal. Return the almonds to the food processor along with the flour, cinnamon, agave nectar, and canola oil. Pulse to combine all the ingredients. Roll the dough into walnut-size balls and place on the prepared baking sheets. Using your thumb, press an indentation into the center of each ball. Fill the indentations with preserves. Bake for 10 to 12 minutes, until golden. Let cool 10 minutes on the baking sheets, then transfer to cooling racks to cool completely.

PB&J Cookies

MAKES | 1½ DOZEN COOKIES   ✹ VEGAN

A great treat for children of all ages. Who can resist PB&J? For peanut allergies, substitute soy nut or other nut butter of your choice. For gluten allergies, replace the spelt flour with garbanzo bean flour. Although not essential, organic peanut butter will offer the best taste and quality.

1 cup sprouted spelt flour

1 cup brown rice flour

2 teaspoons baking power

¼ teaspoon sea salt

½ cup canola oil

½ cup smooth peanut butter

½ cup light agave nectar

1 teaspoon vanilla extract

1 cup juice-sweetened grape
   or strawberry jam or jelly

Preheat the oven to 350°F. Line 2 baking sheets with parchment paper.

Combine the spelt flour, rice flour, baking powder, and salt in a large bowl. In a separate bowl, whisk together the canola oil, peanut butter, agave nectar, and vanilla extract. Add the whisked ingredients to the dry ingredients until well incorporated.

To make large cookies, take a heaping tablespoon of dough and roll it into a ball with the palms of your hands. Place on 1 of the prepared baking sheets and flatten slightly. Using your thumb, press an indentation into the center of the cookie. Fill the center with 1 teaspoon of the jam. Repeat with the remaining dough. Bake for 12 to 15 minutes, until golden. Transfer to cooling racks to cool completely.

Vanilla Crisps

MAKES | 2 DOZEN COOKIES   ⚙ VEGAN

These irresistible cookies are so versatile. For something special, fill them with peanut butter and juice-sweetened jam to make a cookie sandwich. Dip half the sandwich in chocolate ganache and place on waxed paper–lined baking sheets to firm up the chocolate. There's only one word for this—outrageous.

1 cup whole wheat pastry flour
½ cup arrowroot powder
1 teaspoon baking powder
½ teaspoon sea salt
6 tablespoons canola oil
2 tablespoons vanilla extract
½ cup light agave nectar

Preheat the oven to 350°F. Line 2 baking sheets with parchment paper.

In a bowl, mix together the flour, arrowroot powder, baking powder, and salt. In a separate bowl, combine the canola oil, vanilla extract, and agave nectar and whisk together thoroughly. Combine the 2 mixtures until just blended. Drop the batter by the teaspoonful onto the prepared baking sheets. Bake for 7 minutes, or until slightly golden. Do not overbake. Let cool on the baking sheets for 5 minutes, then transfer to cooling racks to cool completely. These cookies crisp up after cooling.

VARIATIONS

Lemon Crisps: Reduce the vanilla extract to 1 tablespoon and add 1 teaspoon lemon extract to the cookie batter.
Almond Crisps: Reduce the vanilla extract to 1 tablespoon and add 1 teaspoon almond extract and ⅓ cup sliced raw almonds to the cookie batter.
DIY Crisps: Create your own special combo by adding ⅓ cup of any (or all) of the following: chopped nuts, dried chopped fruit, or chocolate chips.

Oat 'n' Maple Cream Sandwich Cookies

MAKES | 12 COOKIES ✲ VEGAN

My husband, Joe, asked me to come up with a healthy version of a delicious cookie we once tasted at a gourmet foods shop. I decided to go one better and make them vegan so everyone can love 'em as much as we do.

COOKIES

½ cup nonhydrogenated butter substitute
1 cup light agave nectar
1 teaspoon vanilla extract
½ cup firm silken tofu,
    puréed smooth in a food processor
1 cup sprouted spelt flour
½ teaspoon baking soda
½ teaspoon sea salt
1 teaspoon ground cinnamon
½ teaspoon ground cloves
½ teaspoon ground nutmeg
3 cups regular rolled oats (not quick cooking)
1 cup walnuts, chopped (optional)
1 cup raisins (optional)

FILLING

½ cup nonhydrogenated butter substitute
⅓ cup plus 1 tablespoon light agave nectar
⅓ cup unsweetened soy milk powder
1 teaspoon vanilla extract
1 teaspoon maple extract

Preheat the oven to 350°F. Line 2 baking sheets with parchment paper.

To make the cookies, in a large bowl using an electric mixer set at medium-high speed beat together the butter substitute, agave nectar, and vanilla extract until fluffy, about 1 to 2 minutes. Add the puréed tofu and mix until blended well. Add the flour, baking soda, salt, cinnamon, cloves, nutmeg, and oats and stir well. Fold in the walnuts and raisins if using. Drop the batter by heaping tablespoonfuls onto the prepared baking sheets. Using the back of a spoon, flatten slightly and shape into circles. Bake for 12 to 15 minutes, or until lightly golden. Let cool completely on cooling racks.

To make the filling, in a large bowl using an electric mixer set at medium-high speed beat the butter substitute until softened and fluffy, about 1 to 2 minutes. Add the agave nectar and continue to beat well. Add the soy milk powder, vanilla extract, and maple extract and beat on high, scraping down the bowl to incorporate all the ingredients. Continue to beat until the filling is light and fluffy.

To fill the cookies, spoon 1 or 2 tablespoonfuls of filling on the bottom (flat side) of one cookie. Top with a second cookie, bottom side on the filling. Wrap individually in plastic wrap and refrigerate for up to 5 days or freeze in plastic freezer bags for up to 3 months—providing you have superhuman willpower.

Chewy Double-Chocolate Meringue Cookies

MAKES | 2½ DOZEN COOKIES

A flourless, chocolate lover's dream. These cookies can be stored at room temperature in airtight plastic containers for up to 2 weeks— if they last that long! They will get a bit chewier after the first day but still taste great. Note: Omit the chocolate chips to make these cookies gluten-free.

4 large egg whites, at room temperature
½ teaspoon cream of tartar
¾ cup light agave nectar
½ teaspoon vanilla extract
¼ cup plus 1 tablespoon unsweetened cocoa powder, plus extra for garnish
½ cup grain-sweetened chocolate chips
½ cup walnuts or pecans, coarsely chopped

Preheat the oven to 175°F. Line 2 baking sheets with parchment paper.

Place the egg whites, cream of tartar, and agave nectar in a stainless steel bowl.

Fill a saucepan ¼ full with water and bring to a simmer. Place the mixing bowl containing the egg whites over the simmering water and whisk constantly for about 3 minutes, or until the egg whites are warm. Remove the bowl from the pan and beat the egg whites at low speed with an electric mixer until soft peaks begin to form. Gradually increase the speed to high and beat about 10 minutes, until stiff peaks form. Stir in the vanilla extract. Remove the bowl from the mixer and sift the cocoa powder over the meringue. Sprinkle with chocolate chips and walnuts and gently fold to combine. Drop the meringue mixture by heaping tablespoonfuls onto the prepared baking sheets. Sift a bit of cocoa powder over each cookie and bake for 2 hours. Remove from the oven and let cool completely on the baking sheets before serving.

Classic Chocolate Chip Cookies

MAKES | 2 DOZEN COOKIES

Try this healthy version of America's classic cookie. It has all the rich taste, none of the junk. Your kids will say, "Where's the milk?"

6 tablespoons unsalted butter or nonhydrogenated butter substitute, at room temperature
¾ cup light agave nectar
1 large egg
1 tablespoon vanilla extract
1 cup barley flour
¾ cup oat flour
½ teaspoon baking soda
½ teaspoon sea salt
½ teaspoon ground cinnamon
1 cup grain-sweetened chocolate chips
1 cup pecans, coarsely chopped (optional)

Preheat the oven to 325°F. Line 2 baking sheets with parchment paper.

In a large bowl, beat the butter with an electric mixer until creamy. Add the agave nectar and beat until fluffy, about 1 to 2 minutes. Add the egg and vanilla extract and beat until combined.

In a separate bowl, combine the barley flour, oat flour, baking soda, salt, and cinnamon. Add the dry mixture to the butter mixture and combine well. Fold in the chocolate chips and pecans. Drop by heaping tablespoonfuls onto the prepared baking sheets and press down slightly. Bake the cookies for 12 to 14 minutes, until lightly golden. Do not overbake.

Let cool 5 minutes on the baking sheets, then transfer to cooling racks to cool completely.

Almond Meringue Cookies with Chocolate Orange Ganache Filling

MAKES | 2 DOZEN COOKIES

⚙ GLUTEN-FREE

These cookies were one of the favorites among my testers because the almond meringue creates a delicately crisp cookie that is awesome on its own. Filling them with chocolate ganache takes them to a new level of sophistication.

COOKIES

5 large egg whites
¼ teaspoon cream of tartar
¾ cup light agave nectar
½ teaspoon vanilla extract
1½ cups almond meal

FILLING

¾ cup light agave nectar
½ cup heavy cream or soy creamer
6 ounces unsweetened chocolate, chopped
1 teaspoon vanilla extract
½ teaspoon orange extract

Preheat the oven to 200°F. Line 2 baking sheets with parchment paper.

To make the cookies, in a large bowl using an electric mixer combine the egg whites and cream of tartar, beating on medium speed until soft peaks form, about 1 minute. Gradually add the agave nectar and beat about 2 to 3 minutes, or until firm. Beat in the vanilla extract and fold in the almond meal. Place a medium star tip on a pastry bag and fill with batter. Pipe the meringue into 2-inch round filled circles onto the prepared baking sheets. Bake the cookies about 15 minutes, or until slightly golden. Turn off the heat and let the cookies cool in the oven for 4 hours or overnight. Store unfilled cookies at room temperature for several weeks in sealed plastic containers. Filled cookies are best served soon after filling them, otherwise they become soft (some people love them this way).

To make the filling, heat the agave nectar and cream in a small saucepan. Place the chocolate into a bowl and pour the hot cream over it. Whisk together until smooth and the chocolate is melted. Stir in the vanilla extract and orange extract. Let the ganache cool completely.

To fill the cookies, spread the ganache on the bottom (flat side) of a cookie. Top with a second cookie, bottom side on the filling. Repeat with the remaining cookies.

Cranberry Oat Jumbles

MAKES | 2 DOZEN COOKIES   ✻ VEGAN

These chewy low-fat cookies make the perfect afternoon snack. Chock-full of fiber and protein, they're a nutritious pick-me-up— and they're quick and easy to make.

¼ cup canola oil

¾ cup light agave nectar

¼ cup firm silken tofu

1 tablespoon vanilla extract

¼ teaspoon almond extract

1 cup sprouted spelt flour

1 cup regular rolled oats
   (not quick cooking)

¼ cup ground flaxseeds

½ teaspoon baking soda

½ teaspoon sea salt

1 teaspoon ground cinnamon

½ cup juice-sweetened dried cranberries

¼ cup sunflower seeds

¼ cup raw pumpkin seeds

Preheat the oven to 325°F. Line 2 baking sheets with parchment paper.

Place the canola oil, agave nectar, tofu, vanilla extract, and almond extract in a food processor and blend until smooth, about 2 minutes. In a large bowl, combine the flour, oats, flaxseeds, baking soda, salt, and cinnamon. Add the tofu mixture to the dry ingredients and mix well. Stir in the cranberries, sunflower seeds, and pumpkin seeds. Drop by tablespoonfuls onto the prepared baking sheets. Bake for 10 to 15 minutes, until lightly browned. Cool on cooling racks.

Zucchini Pecan Drops

MAKES | 5 DOZEN SMALL COOKIES

I created this cookie recipe as a way to sneak some veggies into my daughter Sofia's diet when she went through the "I'm not eating any vegetables" stage. She loved them then and still adores them, zucchini and all. These moist, soft cookies are low-fat, high fiber, and a perfect not-too-sweet treat. They also freeze well.

2½ cups sprouted spelt flour
½ cup ground flaxseeds
1 teaspoon baking powder
1½ teaspoons baking soda
1 teaspoon ground allspice
1 teaspoon ground cinnamon
½ teaspoon ground nutmeg
¼ cup canola oil
⅓ cup light agave nectar
4 large egg whites, beaten lightly
2 teaspoons vanilla extract
2 cups finely grated zucchini
   (about 2 medium zucchini)
¾ cup currants
½ cup pecans, chopped

Preheat the oven to 325°F. Line 2 baking sheets with parchment paper.

In a large bowl, combine the flour, flaxseeds, baking powder, baking soda, allspice, cinnamon, and nutmeg. In a separate bowl, whisk together the canola oil, agave nectar, egg whites, vanilla extract, and zucchini. Add the wet ingredients to the dry ingredients and mix well. Stir in the currants and pecans. Drop the batter by heaping teaspoonfuls onto the prepared baking sheets. Bake for 12 to 15 minutes, until slightly golden. Remove from the oven and let cool for 5 minutes. Transfer to cooling racks to cool completely.

Cinnamon Apple Crumb Bars

MAKES | 16 (2- BY 3-INCH) BARS

A cross between apple pie and crumb cake, these cookie bars are perfect for parties, picnics, and crowds, and a great addition to any cookie platter. For the best taste and texture, I recommend you use any combination of Macintosh, Cortland, or Golden Delicious apples for the filling.

CRUST

1 cup regular rolled oats (not quick cooking)
1¼ cups sprouted spelt flour
½ teaspoon baking powder
½ teaspoon sea salt
½ cup canola oil
⅓ cup light agave nectar
1 large egg, beaten

FILLING

5 large apples, peeled, cored, and sliced
⅓ cup light agave nectar
1 teaspoon ground cinnamon
¼ teaspoon ground nutmeg
¼ cup arrowroot powder
Juice of ½ lemon

TOPPING

1 cup regular rolled oats (not quick cooking)
⅔ cup sprouted spelt flour
½ teaspoon ground cinnamon
¼ teaspoon sea salt
½ cup unsalted butter or nonhydrogenated butter substitute, cold, cut into pieces
½ cup light agave nectar

Preheat the oven to 325°F. Lightly oil a 10- by 15- by 1-inch jelly roll pan with canola oil spray.

In a bowl, prepare the crust by combining the oats, flour, baking powder, and salt. Stir in the canola oil, agave nectar, and egg. Spread the mixture evenly in the prepared baking pan.

Prepare the filling by tossing the apples with the agave nectar, cinnamon, nutmeg, arrowroot powder, and lemon juice. Spread the filling evenly over the bottom crust.

Make the crumb topping by mixing the oats, flour, cinnamon, and salt in a bowl. Add the butter pieces and cut into the flour using your fingers or a pastry blender. Add the agave nectar and mix together. The topping will be thick and sticky. Sprinkle the crumb topping evenly over the apples, all the way to the edges of the pan.

Bake for 40 minutes, or until the topping is golden and the apples are tender. Let cool in the pan for 15 to 20 minutes before cutting into bars.

Apricot Butter Bars

MAKES | 24 (2-INCH) BARS   ☼ VEGAN

For variety, substitute prunes for
the apricots in these fat-free (and
guilt-free) bars. Sweet and chewy,
they make a nice lunch box treat.

FILLING

2 cups dried unsulfured apricots

2 cups water

DOUGH

1¾ cups regular rolled oats
    (not quick cooking)

2 cups crispy brown rice cereal

1½ cups sprouted spelt flour or
    whole wheat pastry flour

1 teaspoon baking soda

2 teaspoons ground cinnamon

½ teaspoon ground nutmeg

½ teaspoon cream of tartar

¾ cup light agave nectar

1 cup unsweetened apple juice

1 teaspoon vanilla extract

1 teaspoon almond extract

½ cup sliced raw almonds,
    for topping

To make the filling, place the apricots
and water in a heavy saucepan. Bring to a
boil, then decrease the heat to simmer and
cook partially covered for 20 to 25 minutes,
until the apricots are very soft. Purée the
apricots with the remaining cooking water
using an immersible blender or food processor. Set aside.

Preheat the oven to 350°F. Lightly oil
a 9- by 13-inch baking dish with canola
oil spray.

To make the dough, in a large bowl combine the oats, cereal, flour, baking soda,
cinnamon, nutmeg, and cream of tartar.
In a separate bowl, combine the agave
nectar, apple juice, vanilla extract, and
almond extract. Pour the wet ingredients
into the dry mixture and stir well to combine. Firmly press 2 cups of the dough into
the bottom of the prepared pan. Spread
the filling evenly on top. Mix the sliced
almonds into the remaining dough and
crumble over the top of the filling. Press
down the crumble topping slightly. Bake
for 25 minutes, or until golden. Let cool
in the pan for about 20 minutes before
cutting into squares.

Pecan Pie Squares

MAKES | 16 (2-INCH) BARS

Pecan pie is usually off-limits to me: it's full of corn syrup, which nutritionally speaking is a recipe for disaster. These Pecan Pie Squares, served warm, have the same rich, nutty taste with a fraction of the fat and no refined sugars.

CRUST

½ cup unsalted butter or nonhydrogenated butter substitute, melted
1 cup sprouted spelt flour
½ teaspoon baking soda
Pinch of sea salt
3 tablespoons light agave nectar

TOPPING

1¼ cups amber agave nectar
2 large eggs, beaten
¼ teaspoon sea salt
3 tablespoons unsalted butter or nonhydrogenated butter substitute, melted
½ cup pecans, ground to a meal in a food processor
½ cup pecan halves
2 teaspoons vanilla extract
½ teaspoon ground cinnamon
1½ tablespoons sprouted spelt flour

Preheat the oven to 350°F. Oil an 8- by 8-inch baking pan with canola oil spray.

To make the crust, mix all the crust ingredients together in a bowl with your fingers and press into the prepared pan. Bake for 5 minutes, then remove from the oven. Increase oven temperature to 400°F.

Meanwhile, to make the topping, whisk all the topping ingredients together in a large bowl until well blended. Spread evenly over the prepared crust. Bake for 5 minutes, then reduce oven temperature to 350°F and bake for an additional 12 to 15 minutes, until firm. Let cool 10 to 15 minutes before cutting into squares.

Fluffy Lemon Bars

MAKES | 16 (2-INCH) BARS

I love all things lemon. The barley and oat flours used in this recipe create a nutty crust that complements the tart, soufflélike topping—perfect with a cup of green tea.

CRUST

¼ cup oat flour

¼ cup barley flour

1 cup raw almonds, ground to
    a fine meal in a food processor

¼ cup light agave nectar

1 teaspoon ground cinnamon

1 tablespoon canola oil

TOPPING

1 tablespoon unsalted butter,
    at room temperature

⅔ cup light agave nectar

2 large egg yolks

Juice and freshly grated zest
    of 2 lemons

½ cup barley flour

1 cup evaporated skim milk

3 large egg whites

Preheat the oven to 350°F. Lightly oil an 8- by 8-inch baking pan with canola oil spray.

To make the crust, mix all the crust ingredients together in bowl. Press the crust mixture into the prepared baking pan and bake for 15 minutes, or until slightly browned. Set aside.

To make the topping, in a large bowl whisk together the butter, agave nectar, and egg yolks. Add the lemon juice, lemon zest, flour, and evaporated milk. Whisk until well blended. In a separate bowl, beat the egg whites with an electric mixer set on medium speed for approximately 1 to 2 minutes, until stiff (but not dry) peaks form. Gently fold the egg whites into the lemon mixture until combined. Pour the mixture over the prepared crust and bake for 25 to 30 minutes, until the top begins to turn golden and the filling is set. Remove from the oven and cool on a cooling rack completely before cutting into bars. Store covered in the refrigerator.

Crispy Brown Rice and Cashew Treats

MAKES | 24 (2-INCH) SQUARES   ✦ VEGAN

This is my cleaned-up version of those legendary rice crispy squares. The difference is that these are full of whole grain goodness and nutrients from the nuts and fruit. Try these out on your kids for a guaranteed hit. You can find nut butter at any health food store. Note: Make these gluten-free by using crispy brown rice cereal not sweetened with barley malt.

1 cup light agave nectar
6 tablespoons cashew and macadamia
    nut butter or raw almond butter
Pinch of sea salt
½ teaspoon ground cinnamon
2 tablespoons vanilla extract
8 cups (one 10-ounce box) unsweetened
    crispy brown rice cereal
1 cup unsulfured apricots, chopped
1 cup cashews, toasted and chopped

Lightly oil a 9- by 13-inch glass baking pan with canola oil spray.

In a large bowl, combine the agave nectar, nut butter, salt, cinnamon, and vanilla extract. Mix until well blended. Add the cereal, apricots, and cashews and mix well. Firmly press the mixture into the prepared baking pan and cover with plastic wrap. Refrigerate for 2 or more hours, or until firm. Cut into squares to serve.

Ultimate Fudgy Brownies

MAKES | 24 (2-INCH) BARS

The key to really moist, fudgy brownies is not to overmix the batter. For extra decadence, lightly frost them with softened chocolate ganache (page 108) and sprinkle with extra toasted nuts on top. These treats are for serious chocolate lovers.

6 ounces unsweetened chocolate

1 cup unsalted butter or
   nonhydrogenated butter substitute

4 large eggs

1½ cups light agave nectar

2 teaspoons vanilla extract

1 cup sprouted spelt flour

½ teaspoon baking powder

¼ teaspoon salt

¾ cup pecans or walnuts,
   chopped (optional)

Preheat the oven to 350°F. Lightly oil a 9- by 13-inch baking pan with canola oil spray.

In a glass bowl, combine the chocolate and butter. Microwave on high setting for 2 minutes. Immediately remove from the microwave and stir until the chocolate is completely melted. In a large bowl, lightly beat the eggs with a wire whisk. Add the agave nectar and vanilla extract. Stir in the melted chocolate mixture. Sift the flour, baking powder, and salt over the chocolate mixture. Gently fold the ingredients, just until the flour is incorporated. Gently fold in the pecans. Be sure not to overmix; the mixture will be lumpy.

Pour into the prepared baking pan. Bake for 30 minutes, or until just set. Do not overbake, or the brownies will lose their fudginess. Let cool in the pan before cutting into bars.

The Amazing
Black Bean Brownies

MAKES | 45 (2-INCH) BROWNIES

✹ GLUTEN-FREE

Without exception, this was the most sought-after recipe at my restaurant and bakery. You would never believe these incredibly fudgy brownies are made with beans but no flour. The beans provide great body and fiber without a "beany" taste. Keep the brownies in the refrigerator. They will slice much better if refrigerated several hours or overnight. Find natural coffee substitute at natural food stores.

4 ounces unsweetened chocolate

1 cup unsalted butter or nonhydrogenated
   butter substitute

2 cups soft-cooked black beans,
   drained well

1 cup walnuts, chopped

1 tablespoon vanilla extract

¼ cup natural coffee substitute
   (or instant coffee, for gluten-sensitive)

¼ teaspoon sea salt

4 large eggs

1½ cups light agave nectar

Preheat the oven to 325°F. Line an 9- by 13-inch baking pan with parchment paper and lightly oil with canola oil spray.

Melt the chocolate and butter in a glass bowl in the microwave for 1½ to 2 minutes on high. Stir with a spoon to melt the chocolate completely. Place the beans, ½ cup of the walnuts, the vanilla extract, and a couple of spoonfuls of the melted chocolate mixture into the bowl of a food processor. Blend about 2 minutes, or until smooth. The batter should be thick and the beans smooth. Set aside.

In a large bowl, mix together the remaining ½ cup walnuts, remaining melted chocolate mixture, coffee substitute, and salt. Mix well and set aside.

In a separate bowl, with an electric mixer beat the eggs until light and creamy, about 1 minute. Add the agave nectar and beat well. Set aside.

Add the bean/chocolate mixture to the coffee/chocolate mixture. Stir until blended well. Add the egg mixture, reserving about ½ cup. Mix well. Pour the batter into the prepared pan. Using an electric mixer, beat the remaining ½ cup egg mixture until light and fluffy. Drizzle over the brownie batter. Use a wooden toothpick to pull the egg mixture through the batter, creating a marbled effect. Bake for 30 to 40 minutes, until the brownies are set. Let cool in the pan completely before cutting into squares. (They will be soft until refrigerated.)

Chocolate Raspberry Macaroon Bars

MAKES | 24 (2-INCH) BARS

Chocolate and raspberry are a match made in heaven. Sweet and decadent, these bars are perfect with coffee or espresso.

½ cup unsalted butter or nonhydrogenated
   butter substitute
3 ounces unsweetened chocolate
1½ cups light agave nectar
2 large eggs
2½ teaspoons vanilla extract
1¼ cups whole wheat pastry flour
½ cup juice-sweetened red raspberry jam
½ teaspoon orange extract, or
   1 tablespoon Grand Marnier, or both
4 large egg whites
¼ teaspoon salt
2 tablespoons cocoa powder plus
   extra for dusting
1½ cups almond meal

Preheat the oven to 325°F. Lightly oil a 9- by 13-inch glass baking pan with canola oil spray.

Heat the butter and chocolate in a glass bowl in the microwave on high for 1½ minutes, or until melted. Remove from the microwave and whisk together until the chocolate melts completely, then whisk in ¾ cup of the agave nectar, the eggs, and 2 teaspoons of the vanilla extract until well blended. Next, whisk in the flour. Pour into the prepared pan and bake for 15 minutes, or until the crust is set. Remove from the oven. Increase oven temperature to 350°F.

In a small bowl, mix together the raspberry jam with the orange extract. Spread evenly over the chocolate crust.

In a large bowl, using an electric mixer, beat the egg whites with the remaining ½ teaspoon vanilla extract until slightly thickened, about 1 minute. Add the remaining ¾ cup agave nectar and salt. Beat at medium to high speed until fluffy but not dry, about 30 seconds. Add the cocoa powder and almond meal. Beat until well blended. Pour the mixture over the raspberry jam layer and bake for 20 to 25 minutes, until the top is set. Let cool in the pan, then cut into bars. Sift extra cocoa powder over the bars before serving if desired.

Coconut Chocolate Chip Bars

MAKES | 24 (2-INCH) BARS

Bananas are the surprise ingredient in these yummy, coconutty treats. Substitute cashews or pecans for the walnuts for some great flavor variations.

CRUST

½ cup unsalted butter or
  nonhydrogenated butter substitute
1⅓ cups whole wheat pastry flour
  or sprouted whole wheat flour
Pinch of sea salt

FILLING

2 large eggs, beaten
½ cup light agave nectar
2 teaspoons vanilla extract
2 tablespoons whole wheat pastry flour
  or sprouted whole wheat flour
½ teaspoon sea salt
3 ripe bananas, mashed
¾ cup walnuts
1 cup grain-sweetened chocolate chips
  or carob chips
1 cup dried unsweetened coconut

Preheat the oven to 350°F.
    To make the crust, use an electric mixer to cream together the butter, flour, and salt. Pat into a 9- by 13-inch unoiled baking pan. Bake for 10 minutes and remove. To make the filling, mix all the filling ingredients together and pour over the crust. Bake for 20 to 25 minutes or until slightly golden. Cool completely in the pan before cutting into bars. Keep refrigerated.

Date Nut Squares

MAKES | 16 (2-INCH) SQUARES ⚙ VEGAN

These are my all-time favorite bars; I just love dates and nuts together. These bars have a crumbly texture with a creamy date center enhanced by raspberry juice.

FILLING

2 cups pitted dates, chopped

1 cup raisins

2 teaspoons vanilla extract

1¼ cups raspberry or berry-blend 100 percent fruit juice

CRUST AND TOPPING

2 cups walnuts

½ cup oat flour

½ cup barley flour

2 teaspoons ground cinnamon

⅓ cup light agave nectar

¼ cup canola oil

Preheat the oven to 350°F. Lightly oil an 8-inch square baking pan with canola oil spray.

To make the filling, place the dates, raisins, vanilla extract, and juice in a saucepan and bring to a boil. Decrease the heat and simmer, stirring occasionally, for 5 minutes, or until the liquid has been absorbed and the dates have formed a purée. Set aside.

Grind 1 cup of the walnuts in a food processor until fine. Chop the remaining walnuts by hand until medium coarse. Place all the walnuts in a bowl. Add the oat flour, barley flour, and cinnamon. Mix well. In a separate bowl, stir together the agave nectar and canola oil. Pour over the flour mixture and combine with a fork or your fingers, until crumbly.

Sprinkle slightly more than one half of the crumb mixture into the prepared baking dish. Pat down evenly to form the bottom crust. Spread the date purée over the crumb mixture and top with the remaining crumb mixture. Press down lightly. Bake for 25 minutes, or until golden. Cool for 30 minutes before cutting into squares.

Peanut Butter Energy Bars

MAKES | 24 (2-INCH) BARS

I'm not a fan of commercial protein bars. In my opinion, they're too sweet, more like candy than food. But I do love the idea of portable snacks packed with nutrition. So I decided to make my own and fill them with lots of protein, fiber, and a mild sweetness derived from agave nectar and dried fruit. All my gym buddies love them. They're a great on-the-go snack or even breakfast in a pinch. Substitute almond butter for the peanut butter to change it up a bit.

½ cup oat bran
½ cup oat flour
1 cup sugar-free vanilla whey
    protein powder
¼ cup ground flaxseeds
½ teaspoon sea salt
12 ounces firm silken tofu
½ cup light agave nectar
½ cup smooth or chunky peanut butter
4 large egg whites, beaten
1 teaspoon vanilla extract
½ cup dried unsulfured apricots, chopped
½ cup dried unsweetened cherries, chopped
½ cup dried juice-sweetened blueberries

Preheat the oven to 325°F. Line a 9- by 13-inch baking pan with parchment paper and spray lightly with canola oil spray.

Combine the oat bran, oat flour, whey, flaxseeds, and salt in a large bowl. Set aside.

In a food processor, blend the tofu, agave nectar, peanut butter, egg whites, and vanilla extract until creamy and smooth, about 1 to 2 minutes. Pour over the dry ingredients and stir well to combine. Fold in the apricots, cherries, and blueberries. Spread the mixture in the prepared baking pan and bake for 25 to 30 minutes, until lightly golden. Remove from the oven and let cool completely in the pan before cutting into bars.

Cakes and Cupcakes

Vanilla Sponge Cake with Mango Custard Filling

SERVES | 12

This is a whole grain, sugar-free version of a classic sponge cake. It's light, contains no butter or oil, and freezes wonderfully. You can make the pastry cream up to 3 days in advance.

6 large eggs, separated

3 tablespoons lukewarm water

½ cup light agave nectar

Freshly grated zest of ½ lemon (optional)

2 teaspoons vanilla extract

1⅔ cups sprouted spelt flour

1½ teaspoons baking powder

Vanilla Pastry Cream (page 111)

1 large ripe mango, peeled and
   cut into small dice

Agave Nectar Whipped Cream (page 113)

Preheat the oven to 350°F. Lightly oil two 9-inch layer cake pans with canola oil spray.

In a large bowl, using an electric mixer beat the egg yolks, water, ¼ cup of the agave nectar, the lemon zest, and vanilla extract for 5 minutes, or until pale and creamy. In a separate bowl, using clean beaters beat the egg whites at medium speed until stiff, slowly adding the remaining ¼ cup agave nectar. Continue to beat until stiff and glossy, but not dry, about 1 to 2 minutes.

Carefully fold the egg whites into the egg yolk mixture. In another bowl, sift the flour and baking powder together. Gently fold into the egg mixture. Pour the batter into the prepared pans and bake for 20 to 25 minutes, until a toothpick inserted into the centers of the layers comes out clean. Cool in the pans for 5 minutes, then invert on a cooling rack and cool completely before frosting.

To assemble, spread a generous layer of vanilla pastry cream on the first cake layer. Next add the mango, followed by a bit more pastry cream to anchor the top layer in place. Top with the second layer and frost the entire cake with whipped cream. Refrigerate until ready to serve.

VARIATIONS

Zesty Lemon: Flavor the cake with 2 teaspoons lemon zest and substitute a teaspoon of lemon extract for the vanilla extract. Fill with lemon curd (page 66) and frost with Agave Nectar Whipped Cream (page 113) and sliced fresh strawberries.

Tipsy Mousse: Drizzle the cake layers with your favorite liqueur or rum. Fill with Light Chocolate Mousse (page 101). Frost with Agave Nectar Whipped Cream (page 113) and drizzle on melted chocolate ganache frosting (page 108).

Celebration Cake: Vanilla Buttercream Frosting (page 106) is a classic. Try some sliced bananas inside along with the buttercream or Orange Crème Filling (page 113).

Pineapple Right-Side-Up Cake: One of my favorites is Pineapple Cake Filling (page 115) and fresh whipped cream frosting.

Golden Vanilla Cupcakes with Raspberry Buttercream Frosting

SERVES | 9 (MAKES 9 CUPCAKES)

✹ GLUTEN-FREE

The hardest recipe for me to develop was a really light yellow cake that was still nutritious, moist, and delicious. Well, here it is, and it's gluten-free to boot. Without the food coloring, the frosting will be a pale lavender color.

CUPCAKES

⅓ cup canola oil
½ cup light agave nectar
2 large eggs
¼ cup nonfat plain yogurt
   mixed with ¼ cup water
2 teaspoons vanilla extract
2 teaspoons freshly grated lemon zest
   (about ½ lemon)
1 cup garbanzo bean flour
⅓ cup potato starch
3 tablespoons tapioca flour
1 teaspoon xanthan gum
½ teaspoon baking powder
½ teaspoon baking soda
¼ teaspoon sea salt

FROSTING

½ cup unsalted butter
⅓ cup and 2 tablespoons light agave nectar
½ cup juice-sweetened seedless raspberry jam
1 cup nonfat dry milk
½ teaspoon vanilla extract
A few drops natural red food coloring (optional)

Fresh raspberries for garnish (optional)

Preheat the oven to 325°F. Line a cupcake pan with 9 paper liners and fill the empty cups half full of water to prevent scorching.

To prepare the cupcakes, using an electric mixer beat together the canola oil, agave nectar, and eggs. Add the yogurt mixture, vanilla extract, and lemon zest. Beat again.

Mix the garbanzo bean flour, potato starch, tapioca flour, xanthan gum, baking powder, baking soda, and salt in a large bowl. Slowly add the flour mixture to the yogurt mixture and mix on low speed until just combined. Spoon the batter into the prepared cupcake pan and bake for 20 minutes, or until a toothpick inserted into the center of a cupcake comes out clean. Cool the cupcakes completely on a cooling rack.

To prepare the frosting, use an electric mixer to beat the butter until smooth. Add the agave nectar and beat again until fluffy. Add the raspberry jam and beat well. Add the dry milk, vanilla extract, and food coloring if using. Beat on high speed until light and fluffy, scraping down the bowl as necessary. You will have about 2 cups of frosting.

Frost the cooled cupcakes liberally and garnish with fresh raspberries if desired.

Dark Chocolate Cake

SERVES | 12

You'll go to this recipe again and again when you want a classic chocolate cake.

4 ounces unsweetened chocolate, chopped

¾ cup canola oil

2 cups sprouted spelt flour or
   whole wheat pastry flour

⅓ cup unsweetened cocoa powder

1 teaspoon sea salt

2 teaspoons baking powder

2 teaspoons baking soda

1½ cups light agave nectar

3 large eggs

2 teaspoons vanilla extract

⅓ cup nonfat plain yogurt

3 cups coarsely puréed zucchini
   (about 3 medium zucchini)

Dark Chocolate Ganache Frosting (page 108)

Preheat the oven to 350°F. Lightly oil two 9-inch cake pans with canola oil spray and sprinkle lightly with flour.

Combine the chocolate and ¼ cup of the canola oil in a glass bowl and microwave for about 1½ minutes. Stir to melt the chocolate. Sift together the flour, cocoa powder, salt, baking powder, and baking soda in a large bowl. In a separate bowl, using an electric mixer beat the remaining ½ cup canola oil and the agave nectar. Add the eggs 1 at a time and beat well. Add the melted chocolate and vanilla extract and beat. On low speed, add the flour mixture and the yogurt and mix just until combined. Fold in the zucchini. Pour the batter into the prepared pans. Bake for 35 to 40 minutes, until a toothpick inserted into the centers of the layers comes out clean. Let cool in the pans for 10 minutes, then invert onto cooling racks to cool completely.

To assemble, top the first cake layer with the filling of your choice. Spoon slightly warm ganache over the top and sides of the cake, smoothing it out with an offset spatula or knife. When completely covered, let the ganache firm up in the refrigerator for about ½ hour before slicing the cake.

VARIATIONS

Chocolate Bungalow Cake: Fill with Vanilla Pastry Cream (page 111), and fresh strawberries or bananas, or both. Frost with whipped cream.

Peanut Butter and Chocolate Cake: Fill with peanut butter mousse filling (page 51).

Black Forest Cake: Fill with Sweet Cherry Filling (page 115) and frost with ganache frosting (page 108). Serve with fresh whipped cream.

Chocolate Hazelnut Cake: Fill with Light Chocolate Mousse (page 101). Add a teaspoon of hazelnut extract to ganache and garnish with chopped toasted hazelnuts.

Flourless Chocolate Cake

SERVES | 12 ✿ GLUTEN-FREE

I think this is my favorite chocolate dessert. It has all my favorites: it's chocolate, it's warm, and it's great with ice cream. The combination of dense, not-too-sweet chocolate cake with tangy raspberry sauce and creamy cool ice cream can't be beaten. Use an excellent quality chocolate since it's the main event here.

½ cup unsalted butter,
    cut into small pieces
8 ounces unsweetened chocolate,
    chopped into small pieces
5 large eggs, separated
Pinch of sea salt
1 cup light agave nectar
1 teaspoon vanilla extract
Raspberry Sauce (page 116),
    Hot Fudge Sauce (page 107), and/or
    Hot Buttered Rum Sauce (page 116)
Agave Nectar Whipped Cream (page 113),
    Sinfully Rich Vanilla Bean Ice Cream
    (page 82), or Skinny Vanilla Bean
    Frozen Yogurt (page 83), for garnish
    (optional)

Preheat the oven to 325°F. Lightly oil a 10-inch round cake pan with canola oil spray.

Place the butter and chocolate in a double boiler and melt over lightly simmering water, or microwave in a glass bowl for 2 minutes on medium setting. Stir well to melt the chocolate.

In a separate bowl, whisk together the egg yolks, salt, ¾ cup of the agave nectar, and the vanilla extract. Stir in melted chocolate. Set aside.

With an electric mixer, beat the egg whites on medium speed until soft peaks form, about 1 to 2 minutes. Gradually drizzle in the remaining ¼ cup agave nectar and continue to beat the egg whites until stiff and glossy, but not dry, approximately 1 to 2 minutes. Gently fold the egg whites into the chocolate mixture until no white streaks remain. Pour into the prepared pan and bake for about 1 hour and 15 minutes, until cake is set. Remove from the oven and turn out the cake onto a large plate. Carefully invert again onto a cooling rack so that the top side is up. Cool until just warm. Slide the cake onto a serving plate using 2 large spatulas.

Serve warm with any combination of sauce, whipped cream, and ice cream.

Fudgy Chocolate Cupcakes

SERVES | 12 (MAKES 12 CUPCAKES)

✺ GLUTEN-FREE

One of my favorite grains to eat is quinoa. It contains all the amino acids required to make a complete protein. Plus, it's high in fiber. In baking, though, the flour can be tricky to work with due to its distinctive flavor. Not in this recipe. The quinoa is no match for the rich chocolate flavor and aroma in this superprotein cupcake that's moist and fudgy. P.S.: They're gluten-free and low-fat, too.

¼ cup unsalted butter or
 nonhydrogenated butter substitute
½ cup water
⅓ cup unsweetened cocoa powder
¾ cup light agave nectar
1¼ cups quinoa flour
½ teaspoon baking powder
½ teaspoon baking soda
½ teaspoon sea salt
2 large eggs, separated
1 teaspoon vanilla extract
¼ cup nonfat plain yogurt or
 unsweetened soy yogurt

Vanilla Buttercream Frosting (page 106),
 Fat-Free Vanilla Yogurt Frosting (page 107),
 Vegan Chocolate Buttercream Frosting
 (page 109), or Vanilla Buttercream Frosting
 (page 106)

Preheat the oven to 375°F. Line a cupcake pan with 12 paper liners.

Place the butter and water in a saucepan. Bring to a boil and remove from heat. Whisk in the cocoa powder and agave nectar. Let cool to room temperature.

In a large bowl, sift together the flour, baking powder, baking soda, and salt. Add the cooled cocoa mixture, egg yolks, vanilla extract, and yogurt to the flour and mix well. In a separate bowl, using an electric mixer at medium speed, beat the egg whites until stiff, but not dry, approximately 2 minutes. Gently fold into the batter.

Spoon the batter into the prepared cupcake pan and bake for 15 to 20 minutes, until a toothpick inserted into the center of a cupcake comes out clean. Frost the cupcakes with the frosting of your choice.

Chocolate Peanut Butter Mousse–Filled Cupcakes

SERVES | 18 (MAKES 18 CUPCAKES)

❀ VEGAN

These vegan cupcakes are very moist and decadent. The peanut butter filling doubles as a cake filling.

CUPCAKES

2¾ cups sprouted spelt flour
   or whole wheat pastry flour
1 teaspoon baking powder
2 teaspoons baking soda
¾ teaspoon sea salt
⅔ cup unsweetened cocoa powder, sifted
½ cup canola oil
1¼ cups light agave nectar
1 cup soy milk
½ cup firm silken tofu
1 tablespoon vanilla extract
2 tablespoons raw apple cider vinegar

FILLING

12 ounces light firm silken tofu
½ cup light agave nectar
1 cup smooth peanut butter
1 tablespoon vanilla extract
½ teaspoon sea salt

Vegan Chocolate Ganache Frosting (page 108)
Chopped toasted peanuts, for garnish (optional)

Preheat the oven to 325°F. Line 2 cupcake pans with 18 paper liners and fill the empty cups half full of water to prevent scorching.

To make the cupcakes, mix the flour, baking powder, baking soda, salt, and cocoa powder together in a large bowl. In a food processor, blend the canola oil, agave nectar, soy milk, tofu, vanilla extract, and vinegar, scraping down the bowl often. Blend until very smooth, with no chunks of tofu visible, about 2 to 3 minutes. Combine the wet ingredients with the dry ingredients. Stir well and spoon into the prepared cupcake pan, leaving some room at the top of each cup. Bake for 20 minutes, or until a toothpick inserted into the center of a cupcake comes out clean. Remove the cupcakes from the pan and place on a cooling rack. Cool completely before filling and frosting.

To prepare the filling, blend the tofu in a food processor until very smooth and creamy, approximately 1 to 2 minutes. Add the agave nectar and blend again. Add the peanut butter, vanilla extract, and salt and blend thoroughly until very light and smooth. Refrigerate for 1 to 2 hours to firm before filling the cupcakes.

To assemble the cupcakes, you will need a pastry bag fitted with a large, plain smooth tip. Fill the pastry bag with peanut butter mousse and insert the tip halfway into the top of a cupcake. Squeeze filling inside each cupcake just until it starts to expand.

Next frost the tops. If the frosting is too firm, heat in the microwave for a few seconds to soften it up. Spread the ganache evenly over the tops of the cupcakes. Let the cupcakes sit in the refrigerator until ready to serve.

Garnish with peanuts if desired.

Mocha Hazelnut Cake

SERVES | 12　✱ GLUTEN-FREE

A most flavorful flourless cake that's airy light in texture but rich and intense in taste.

CAKE

4 large eggs, separated

2 whole eggs

½ cup light agave nectar

1 teaspoon finely grated orange zest

1¼ cups finely ground hazelnuts,
　　raw not toasted, or almond meal

FILLING

12 ounces firm silken tofu

2 tablespoons nonhydrogenated butter
　　substitute, melted

⅓ cup light agave nectar

1 teaspoon unsweetened soy milk

1 tablespoon natural coffee substitute
　　or instant coffee (for gluten-sensitive)

1 tablespoon unsweetened cocoa powder

Pinch of sea salt

½ teaspoon vanilla extract

**Dark Chocolate Ganache Frosting (page 108) or
　　Vegan Chocolate Ganache Frosting (page 108)**

Preheat the oven to 325°F. Lightly oil two 9-inch cake pans with canola oil spray and line the bottoms with parchment paper.

To make the cake, using an electric mixer beat the 4 egg yolks, the 2 whole eggs, 6 tablespoons of the agave nectar, and the orange zest until creamy and pale in color, about 1 to 2 minutes. Gradually stir in the hazelnuts until mixed evenly. In a separate bowl, beat the 4 egg whites at medium high speed until soft peaks form, about 2 minutes. Add the remaining 2 tables-poons agave nectar and beat until slightly stiffer peaks form, another 1 to 2 minutes. (Do not overmix.) Gently fold the beaten egg whites into the hazelnut mixture. Pour the batter into the prepared pans and bake for about 35 minutes, or until a toothpick inserted into the centers of the layers comes out clean. Remove from the oven and let rest for 5 minutes. Invert onto a cooling rack and peel off the parchment paper. Let cool completely.

Prepare the filling by blending the tofu in a food processor until smooth and creamy, about 2 to 3 minutes. Add the butter substitute and agave nectar. Blend again until incorporated. Heat the soy milk in the microwave for 5 seconds, add the coffee substitute, stir to dissolve, and pour into the food processor. Add the cocoa powder, salt, and vanilla extract and blend until all the ingredients are well combined.

To assemble the cake, top the cake layer with the filling and spread evenly with an offset spatula or knife. Top with the second layer and glaze with the ganache frosting by spooning it over the top and sides of the cake, smoothing it out with the spatula.

Carrot Cake

SERVES | 12

You have to have a great carrot cake recipe to go to now and again. This one fits the bill—supermoist and loaded with goodies. Cut back on the fat even further by trying the Fat-Free Vanilla Yogurt Frosting (page 107) on this cake.

3 cups finely grated carrots
 (about 15 medium carrots)
½ cup raisins
½ cup unsweetened shredded coconut
1 cup walnuts, chopped
2 cups sprouted spelt flour, or
 1½ cups barley flour and
 ½ cup oat flour
2 teaspoons baking soda
½ teaspoon baking powder
2 teaspoons ground cinnamon
¾ cup light agave nectar
3 large eggs
½ cup canola oil
1 cup nonfat plain yogurt
2 teaspoons vanilla extract
Cream Cheese Frosting (page 110),
 Vanilla Buttercream Frosting (page 106), or
 Fat-Free Vanilla Yogurt Frosting (page 107)

Preheat the oven to 350°F. Lightly oil two 9-inch cake pans with canola oil spray.

Mix together the carrots, raisins, coconut, and walnuts in a large bowl. In a separate bowl, combine the flour, baking soda, baking powder, and cinnamon. In a food processor, blend the agave nectar, eggs, canola oil, yogurt, and vanilla extract for about 1 minute. Add the egg mixture to the flour mixture and stir to blend. Add the carrot mixture and stir until combined. Pour the batter into the prepared pans and bake for 30 to 35 minutes, until a toothpick inserted into the centers of the layers comes out clean. Let cool in the pan, then invert onto a platter. Frost the cake with your choice of frosting.

Peach Melba Cake

This is a special vegan cake that's an impressive dessert for dinner guests. The custard and fruit make a delightful topping that's fat-free and looks like you toiled for hours over it.

CAKE

1 cup barley flour
½ cup oat flour
1 tablespoon baking powder
¼ cup canola oil
⅓ cup light agave nectar
½ cup unsweetened soy milk
¼ cup firm silken tofu
1½ teaspoons vanilla extract
1 teaspoon freshly grated orange zest

CUSTARD

1½ cups unsweetened soy milk
1 tablespoon agar flakes
1 cup sliced peaches, fresh or frozen
3 tablespoons arrowroot powder
2 teaspoons vanilla extract
⅓ cup light agave nectar

TOPPING

1½ cups fresh strawberries,
   sliced in half lengthwise
1 cup peach nectar (no sugar added)
2 tablespoons light agave nectar
1 tablespoon plus 1 teaspoon agar flakes

Preheat the oven to 325°F. Oil an 8-inch-square baking pan with canola oil spray.

Sift together the barley flour, oat flour, and baking powder. In a food processor, blend the canola oil, agave nectar, soy milk, tofu, vanilla extract, and orange zest until smooth, about 1 to 2 minutes. Stir into the dry ingredients and mix until smooth. Pour into the prepared pan and bake for 15 to 20 minutes, until a toothpick inserted into the center of the cake comes out clean. Let the cake cool in the pan for at least 1 hour.

To prepare the custard, mix the soy milk and agar flakes in a saucepan. Bring to a boil, stirring constantly. Decrease the heat and simmer about 5 to 7 minutes, or until the agar flakes have dissolved, stirring occasionally. Place the peaches, arrowroot powder, vanilla extract, and agave nectar in a food processor and blend until smooth, about 1 minute. Add this to the agar mixture in the saucepan and mix together. Bring to a boil, then decrease the heat to low and simmer until thickened. While still hot, pour the mixture over the cooled cake. Refrigerate for at least 1 hour.

To prepare the topping, arrange the strawberry halves decoratively over the top of the cake. In a saucepan, add the peach nectar, agave nectar, and agar flakes and bring to a boil. Decrease the heat and simmer, stirring often, about 5 to 7 minutes, until the agar flakes have dissolved. Slowly pour the hot nectar mixture over the strawberries on the cake and refrigerate about 1½ to 2 hours.

Banana Daiquiri Cake

SERVES | 18 (MAKES 1 LAYER
CAKE AND 6 CUPCAKES)

This dense moist and delicious cake was a favorite at my restaurant, Sprouts. In scaling down the recipe (which made lots of cakes), I got down to these measurements. You'll have a little batter left over for cupcakes. It's great to freeze them for when the cake is all gone.

1 cup amber agave nectar
¾ cup canola oil
4 large eggs
6 ripe bananas, mashed
2 teaspoons vanilla extract
2 cups barley flour
1¾ cups oat flour
2 teaspoons baking soda
Pinch of sea salt
2 teaspoons ground cinnamon
1 teaspoon ground nutmeg
Rum Cream Cheese Frosting (see page 110)
Toasted coconut or chopped walnuts,
    for garnish (optional)

Preheat the oven to 325°F. Lightly oil two 9-inch cake pans with canola oil spray and lightly dust with flour. Line a cupcake pan with 6 paper liners and fill any empty cups half full of water to prevent scorching.

In a large bowl, using an electric mixer on medium speed, cream the agave nectar, canola oil, eggs, bananas, and vanilla extract.

In a separate bowl, combine the barley flour, oat flour, baking soda, salt, cinnamon, and nutmeg. Add the flour mixture to the banana mixture and blend on low speed until just combined. Pour the batter into the prepared pans and bake the cake layers for 35 to 40 minutes, and the cupcakes for 20 to 25 minutes, until a toothpick inserted into the center of a cupcake comes out clean. Remove from the oven. Let cool in the pans for 5 to 10 minutes, then cool completely on cooling racks. Frost with the cream cheese frosting. Sprinkle some toasted coconut or walnuts over the cream cheese frosting for extra nutty flavor and texture if desired.

Gingerbread Cake with Lemon Crème Topping

SERVES | 12 ✸ VEGAN

This low-fat vegan cake is incredibly delicious served warm from the oven and topped with a cool lemon tofu crème. Using fresh ginger makes a great difference in its taste. I prefer this cake without the nuts and raisins, but others enjoy the texture and sweetness they add. Either way, this flavorful cake is sure to become a favorite of yours.

1 cup barley flour
¾ cup oat flour
2 teaspoons ground cinnamon
½ teaspoon ground allspice
¼ teaspoon ground cloves
1 tablespoon baking powder
12 ounces light firm silken tofu
2 tablespoons canola oil
½ cup amber agave nectar
¼ cup dark molasses
1 tablespoon grated fresh ginger
⅓ cup unsweetened soy milk
½ cup pecans, chopped (optional)
½ cup raisins (optional)
Lemon Tofu Crème (page 114)

Preheat the oven to 350°F. Lightly oil an 8-inch square baking pan with canola oil spray.

Sift the barley flour, oat flour, cinnamon, allspice, cloves, and baking powder together in a large bowl. In a food processor, blend the tofu, canola oil, agave nectar, molasses, and ginger until smooth and creamy, about 1 to 2 minutes. Add the soy milk and blend well. Fold in the pecans and raisins if using. Pour the batter into the prepared pan and bake for 30 minutes, or until a toothpick inserted into the center of the cake comes out clean. Cool on a cooling rack, and serve warm with the lemon crème. This cake must be stored in the refrigerator as tofu can spoil at room temperature.

Lemon Chiffon Cake

SERVES | 12

The texture of this cake is that of angel food cake, but made with whole grains, it has more substance than the white version.

CAKE

1¼ cups sprouted spelt flour
    or whole wheat pastry flour
1 teaspoon vanilla extract
1 teaspoon lemon extract
1 teaspoon freshly grated lemon zest
10 large egg whites
1 teaspoon cream of tartar
¾ cup light agave nectar

FROSTING

½ cup light agave nectar
2 large egg whites
½ teaspoon cream of tartar
1 tablespoon fresh lemon juice
¼ teaspoon lemon extract
½ teaspoon vanilla extract

1 pint fresh blueberries

Preheat the oven to 325°F. Lightly oil the bottom only of a 10-inch tube pan with canola oil spray.

In a large bowl, sift in the flour, then stir in the vanilla extract, lemon extract, and lemon zest.

In a separate bowl, with an electric mixer beat the egg whites on medium speed until frothy. Add the cream of tartar and beat until soft peaks form, about 1 to 2 minutes. Gradually add the agave nectar and increase to high speed. Beat until stiff and glossy, but not dry, about 1 minute. Gently fold the egg whites into the flour mixture. Spoon the batter into the prepared pan. Using a serrated knife, cut though the batter to remove any air bubbles. Bake for 45 minutes, or until a toothpick inserted into the center of the cake comes out clean. Remove from the oven and invert on a cooling rack to cool completely.

To prepare the frosting, in a saucepan bring the agave nectar to a boil over medium heat. Let simmer for 3 to 4 minutes, stirring occasionally, then set aside. In the top of a double boiler, over medium heat, beat the egg whites, cream of tartar, and lemon juice with an electric mixer, or by hand with a balloon whisk, for 4 to 5 minutes, until light and foamy. Slowly drizzle the hot agave nectar into the egg whites, beating constantly for another 4 to 5 minutes, until the frosting is thick. Beat in the lemon extract and vanilla extract and beat 2 minutes more. The frosting should be smooth, fluffy, and of spreading consistency.

When the cake has cooled completely, slice it in half horizontally using a serrated knife. Fill the cake with half the frosting and some blueberries. Top with the other cake half. Spread the remaining frosting on top and garnish with the remaining blueberries. Serve soon after frosting to maintain this cake's light, airy texture.

Hopsie's Cupcakes

SERVES | 12 (MAKES 12 CUPCAKES)

Okay, so why are these called Hopsie's Cupcakes? Because they're made with lots of garden veggies, like zucchini and carrots, and that's what our pet bunny, Hopsie, loves to eat. My daughter, Sofia, told me during our testing of this recipe that these would be great for Hopsie. She, of course, loves them because they're made with the stuff that Hopsie eats.

2 cups packed finely grated zucchini
   (about 2 medium zucchini)
1 cup packed finely grated carrots
   (about 5 or 6 medium carrots)
1 teaspoon sea salt
1½ cups sprouted spelt flour
   or whole wheat pastry flour
1 teaspoon baking powder
1 teaspoon baking soda
1½ teaspoons ground cinnamon
¼ teaspoon ground nutmeg
¾ cup light agave nectar
⅔ cup canola oil
2 large eggs
½ cup walnuts, chopped, plus extra for garnish
   (optional)
⅓ cup currants or raisins (optional)
Cream Cheese Frosting (page 110), Vanilla
   Buttercream Frosting (page 106), or
   Fat-Free Vanilla Yogurt Frosting (page 107)

Place the zucchini and carrots in a strainer. Sprinkle with the salt and mix well. Let drain for 15 to 20 minutes, until most of the moisture is released.

Preheat the oven to 350°F. Line a cupcake pan with 12 paper liners.

In a large bowl, stir together the flour, baking powder, baking soda, cinnamon, and nutmeg.

In a separate bowl, using an electric mixer beat together the agave nectar and canola oil. Add the eggs and beat well. Add the egg mixture to the flour mixture and beat until well combined. Squeeze out any remaining moisture from the drained zucchini and carrots. Using a wooden spoon or rubber spatula, fold in the zucchini, carrots, walnuts, and currants, if using, and spoon the batter into the prepared cupcake pan.

Bake for 20 to 25 minutes, until a toothpick inserted into the center of a cupcake comes out clean. Cool completely on cooling racks before frosting. Sprinkle with extra walnuts if desired.

Spiced Pumpkin Apple Cupcakes

SERVES | 12 (MAKES 12 CUPCAKES)

This is favorite autumn recipe that I like to serve at Halloween or Thanksgiving get-togethers. The little ones just love these moist, spicy cupcakes. They're delicious with fat-free yogurt frosting, too.

¾ cup canned organic pumpkin

2 large eggs

¾ cup amber agave nectar

½ cup canola oil

½ tablespoon vanilla extract

½ teaspoon fresh lemon juice

2 cups sprouted spelt flour, regular whole
   grain spelt flour, or whole wheat pastry flour

½ tablespoon baking powder

½ teaspoon baking soda

2 teaspoons ground cinnamon

¼ teaspoon ground ginger

Pinch of sea salt

2 apples (any variety), peeled
   and chopped into small pieces

Cream Cheese Frosting (page 110)

Toasted walnuts or pecans for garnish
   (optional)

Preheat the oven to 350°F. Line a cupcake pan with 12 paper liners.

In a large bowl, whisk the pumpkin, eggs, agave nectar, canola oil, vanilla extract, and lemon juice until well blended. In a separate bowl, combine the flour, baking powder, baking soda, cinnamon, ginger, and salt. Add the pumpkin mixture to the dry ingredients and mix until just blended. Stir in the apples. Spoon into the prepared cupcake pan and bake for 25 to 30 minutes, until a toothpick inserted into the center of a cupcake comes out clean. Cool the cupcakes in the pan for 10 minutes, then transfer to a cooling rack. When completely cool, frost the cupcakes. Sprinkle toasted walnuts on top of each cupcake if desired.

Strawberry Shortcakes

MAKES | ABOUT 6 SHORTCAKES

A traditional summer treat, especially yummy when strawberries are in season. For the sweetest berries, nothing beats freshly picked. Adjust the amount of agave nectar you use in the filling depending on the sweetness of the berries.

FILLING

1 quart ripe strawberries, rinsed, stemmed, and sliced
¼ to ⅓ cup light agave nectar
½ tablespoon fresh lemon juice
1 tablespoon Grand Marnier liqueur (optional)

SHORTCAKES

2 cups sprouted spelt flour or whole wheat pastry flour
½ tablespoon baking powder
½ teaspoon baking soda
¼ teaspoon sea salt
5 tablespoons frozen unsalted butter, cut into pieces
½ cup nonfat Greek-style plain yogurt
½ cup cold water
2 tablespoons light agave nectar
½ teaspoon vanilla extract
Agave Nectar Whipped Cream (page 113)

To make the filling, mix all the filling ingredients in a bowl and let macerate at room temperature for about 1 hour, or overnight in the refrigerator.

Preheat the oven to 375°F. Line 2 baking sheets with parchment paper.

To make the shortcakes, sift the flour, baking powder, baking soda, and salt together into a large bowl. Cut the butter into the flour using a pastry blender or 2 forks until the mixture resembles a coarse meal. In a small bowl, mix together the yogurt, water, agave nectar, and vanilla extract until smooth. Pour the liquid ingredients into the flour mixture and gently combine with your hands or a wooden spoon to form a rough dough.

Place the dough on a lightly floured work surface and knead 5 to 10 times. Do not overprocess the dough or it will be tough. Pat the dough into a rectangle ¾-inch thick. Using a 3-inch round cookie cutter, cut the dough into biscuits, carefully removing the cutter without twisting (lest the biscuits won't rise as high). Gently press the scraps together to form extra biscuits. Do not knead the dough or the biscuits will not rise. Place the cut biscuits on the prepared baking sheets and bake for 20 minutes, or until golden. Let cool on cooling racks.

To serve, split each shortcake in half horizontally. Generously spoon some strawberry mixture over the bottom half of the biscuit, letting the juices soak in. Top with a dollop of whipped cream and the top half of the biscuit.

Creamy Strawberry Cheesecake

SERVES | 12

I get raves when I make this cheese-cake, and I'm sure you will, too.

CRUST

1 cup whole wheat pastry flour
½ teaspoon sea salt
1 teaspoon baking powder
1 tablespoon nonfat dry milk
6 tablespoons unsalted butter, melted
¼ cup light agave nectar
½ teaspoon vanilla extract
½ teaspoon ground cinnamon

FILLING

16 ounces cream cheese
8 ounces low-fat Neufchâtel cheese
1 cup light agave nectar
4 large eggs, at room temperature,
   beaten until creamy
1 cup nonfat Greek-style plain yogurt
1 tablespoon vanilla extract
2 teaspoons freshly grated lemon zest

TOPPING

1 cup sliced ripe strawberries
½ cup water
½ cup light agave nectar
2 tablespoons fresh lemon juice
1 tablespoon arrowroot powder
1 pint ripe strawberries, halved
Agave Nectar Whipped Cream (page 113)

Preheat the oven to 400°F.

Prepare the crust by mixing together the flour, salt, baking powder, and dry milk in a large bowl. Stir in the butter, agave nectar, vanilla extract, and cinnamon. Mix well and press into the bottom of a 10-inch springform pan. Bake for 5 minutes, or until the crust is set.

To make the filling, beat the cream cheese and Neufchâtel cheese together until smooth. Add the agave nectar and beat until creamy. Add the eggs, yogurt, vanilla extract, and lemon zest. Stir until well combined. Pour the filling into the prebaked crust and bake for 50 to 55 minutes, until set and slightly golden. Remove the cake from the oven and let cool in the pan on a cooling rack for 30 minutes, then refrigerate for 3 hours or more in the pan before serving.

To make the topping, blend the sliced strawberries with the water, agave nectar, and lemon juice in a food processor, until smooth, about 1 minute. Pour all but ½ cup of the mixture into a small saucepan. Cook over medium heat until the mixture begins to simmer. Meanwhile, whisk the arrowroot powder into the remaining ½ cup of the strawberry mixture. Whisk this mixture into the simmering strawberry sauce in the pan, and stir over low heat until thickened, about 1 minute. Remove from the heat, let cool, then refrigerate until cold.

Place the halved strawberries in concentric circles on top of the cake. Spoon the chilled strawberry sauce over the top of the cheesecake. Serve with whipped cream.

Dairy-Free Blueberry Cheesecake

SERVES | 12   ❀ VEGAN

This blueberry topping can also be used over ice cream or yogurt.

CRUST

1 cup sprouted spelt flour or
    whole wheat pastry flour
½ cup ground pecans
1 teaspoon baking powder
½ teaspoon sea salt
6 tablespoons nonhydrogenated
    butter substitute, melted
¼ cup light agave nectar
½ teaspoon vanilla extract
½ teaspoon ground cinnamon

FILLING

18 ounces firm silken tofu
8 ounces soy cream cheese
¼ cup canola oil
Freshly grated zest of 1 lemon
Juice of 2 lemons
¾ cup light agave nectar
½ teaspoon sea salt
¼ cup unsweetened soy milk
2 teaspoons vanilla extract

TOPPING

1 pound fresh or frozen blueberries
¾ cup water
⅓ cup light agave nectar
1 tablespoon fresh lemon juice
2 tablespoons arrowroot powder

Preheat the oven to 350°F. Lightly oil a 10-inch springform pan with canola oil spray.

To make the crust, mix the flour, pecans, baking powder, and salt together in a bowl. Stir in the butter substitute, agave nectar, vanilla extract, and cinnamon. Mix well. Pat into the bottom of the prepared pan. Bake for 8 minutes, or until the crust is set, then set aside.

To make the filling, place the tofu, cream cheese, canola oil, lemon zest, lemon juice, agave nectar, and salt into a food processor. Blend until very smooth and creamy, with the tofu well incorporated, scraping down the bowl often. Add the soy milk and vanilla extract and blend again until very smooth. Pour into the prebaked crust and bake for 30 to 40 minutes, until the cake is firm in the middle. (The cake will continue to set as it cools.) Cool in the pan on a cooling rack for 30 minutes, then refrigerate in the pan for several hours until well chilled.

To prepare the topping, place the blueberries, water, agave nectar, and lemon juice in a saucepan. Cook over medium heat until the mixture comes to a simmer. In a small bowl, dissolve the arrowroot powder in 2 tablespoons cold water and whisk into the blueberry mixture. Cook over low heat, stirring, until the mixture thickens, about 1 minute. Cool to room temperature, then refrigerate the mixture until well chilled and thickened. Spoon the topping on the cheesecake and serve.

Pies, Tarts, and Crisps

Spiced Pumpkin Date Pie

SERVES | 8   ☀ VEGAN

This is a new take on an old favorite. Dates add great flavor and texture to the creamy spiced filling in this vegan pie. The nutty pecan crust is the perfect contrast to the velvety smooth pumpkin filling. Don't wait until Thanksgiving to try this one!

Nut Pastry Crust, made with pecans, unbaked (page 78)
1 (15-ounce) can plain organic pumpkin purée
12 ounces firm silken tofu
¼ cup canola oil
1 cup pitted dates, soaked in hot water for 30 to 40 minutes and drained
½ cup light agave nectar
1 teaspoon ground cinnamon
¼ teaspoon ground cloves
¼ teaspoon ground nutmeg
2 teaspoons vanilla extract
Soy whipped cream, for garnish (optional)

Preheat the oven to 325°F.

Blend the pumpkin, tofu, canola oil, dates, agave nectar, cinnamon, cloves, nutmeg, and vanilla extract in a food processor until very smooth, scraping down the bowl occasionally, about 2 to 3 minutes. Make sure all the dates have been blended well. Pour the filling into the unbaked pie crust and bake for 40 to 45 minutes, until firm and golden. Cool before serving. Soy whipped cream makes a delicious accompaniment.

Coconut Custard Pie

SERVES | 8   ☀ VEGAN

This delicious vegan pie was another wildly popular dessert at my market bakery. The crumbly oat crust goes great with the cool, creamy filling. And, if awesome taste is not enough to tempt you, it's quick and easy to prepare.

Oat Pastry Piecrust, unbaked (page 78)
15 ounces regular firm tofu, drained
12 ounces firm silken tofu
¼ cup canola oil
1 cup light agave nectar
2 tablespoons fresh lemon juice
1½ tablespoons vanilla extract
½ teaspoon lemon extract
½ teaspoon sea salt
1 cup unsweetened shredded coconut, soaked in 1 cup hot water for 15 minutes and drained

Preheat the oven to 350°F.

In a food processor, blend the tofu, silken tofu, canola oil, agave nectar, lemon juice, vanilla extract, lemon extract, and salt, scraping down the bowl often, until very smooth. This will take some time. When the mixture is completely smooth, add the coconut and blend just until combined. Spoon into the unbaked piecrust and bake for 30 to 35 minutes, until the tofu is set. Remove from the oven and let cool to room temperature before refrigerating. The pie gets firmer as it cools in the refrigerator.

Banana Cream Pie

SERVES | 12

Bananas and cream are a perfect combination made even better in a buttery walnut piecrust. Subtly sweet, this pie is a dessert for all seasons.

Nut Pastry Crust, prepared with
   walnuts and prebaked (page 78)
3 large egg yolks
½ cup light agave nectar
3 tablespoons arrowroot powder
Pinch of sea salt
1½ cups low-fat milk
1 tablespoon unsalted butter
1 teaspoon vanilla extract
½ cup heavy cream
3 or 4 ripe but firm bananas, sliced
Agave Nectar Whipped Cream (page 113)
Sliced bananas and toasted walnuts,
   for garnish (optional)

Beat the egg yolks in a heavy saucepan. Add the agave nectar, arrowroot powder, and salt. Beat together well and stir in the milk. Place the pan over medium heat and add the butter. Stir constantly about 5 minutes, until the mixture is thick and bubbly. Remove from the heat and stir in the vanilla extract. Pour the custard into a bowl and cover with plastic wrap that rests gently on the surface of the custard to prevent a skin from forming. Chill for 2 or more hours.

Whip the cream until stiff. Fold into the chilled custard. Spoon approximately ⅓ of the custard into the prebaked piecrust. Layer the sliced bananas and toasted walnuts, if using, over the custard layer and top with the remaining custard. Cover with plastic and refrigerate for at least 6 to 8 hours.

VARIATION

Black Bottom Banana Cream Pie: Drizzle Hot Fudge Sauce (page 107) over the bottom of the prebaked cooled crust to cover thinly. Reserve the remaining sauce for garnish. Let cool in the refrigerator. Proceed with the filling instructions. To serve, lightly drizzle some hot fudge sauce over a pie slice and garnish with chopped toasted walnuts.

Prior to serving, top the pie with whipped cream, mounding it high for dramatic presentation. Garnish with additional bananas and toasted walnuts.

Lemon Meringue Pie

I love lemon desserts. But lemon meringue pie was strictly off-limits to me since typically it's all sugar. Not this one. It features a flaky, tender whole grain crust with a tart and tangy lemon filling topped with mounds of fluffy meringue— and not a single drop of sugar. Truly a lemon lover's dream. The meringue may weep a bit after refrigeration, but this will not affect the taste or texture of the pie.

1 Sweet Pastry Crust, prebaked (page 76)

LEMON CURD

1 cup light agave nectar

6½ tablespoons arrowroot powder

¼ teaspoon sea salt

1½ cups water

4 large egg yolks

¼ cup fresh lemon juice

2 tablespoons freshly grated lemon zest
(about 4 lemons)

2 tablespoons unsalted butter

MERINGUE

5 large egg whites

¼ teaspoon cream of tartar

¼ teaspoon salt

⅓ cup light agave nectar

Preheat the oven to 350°F.

Prepare the filling by combining the agave nectar, arrowroot powder, and salt in a heavy saucepan. Add the water and whisk until smooth. Bring to a slow boil over medium heat, stirring constantly. Boil for about 30 to 60 seconds to thicken and remove from the heat.

In a small bowl, beat the egg yolks with a whisk. While whisking, slowly pour ¼ cup of the hot agave nectar mixture into the yolks and whisk until smooth, tempering the eggs. Then slowly pour the egg mixture into the saucepan, whisking until all is smooth. Stir in the lemon juice, lemon zest, and butter. Bring the mixture to a boil over medium heat, stirring constantly. Simmer to thicken for about 1 minute. Pour the hot mixture into the prebaked piecrust.

To make the meringue, use an electric mixer at low speed to beat the egg whites, cream of tartar, and salt until soft peaks form, about 1 to 2 minutes. Increase the speed to medium and add the agave nectar, 1 tablespoon at a time, and continue beating until stiff but not dry, approximately another 1 to 2 minutes. Spoon the meringue over the pie filling, mounding high in the center and spreading to the crust, making decorative swirls with the spoon.

Bake the pie for 7 minutes, or until the meringue is lightly browned on the edges. Cool on a cooling rack to room temperature, then refrigerate for at least 2 hours before serving.

Guilt-Free Shredded Apple Pie

SERVES | 12

⚙ VEGAN

This refreshing apple pie is made with enzyme-rich raw apples and contains no fat. Completely fat-free, dairy-free, egg-free, sugar-free, and wheat-free— it's totally guilt-free.

CRUST

2 cups regular rolled oats (not quick cooking)
1 cup unsweetened applesauce
¼ teaspoon salt

FILLING

2 cups unsweetened apple juice
¼ cup light agave nectar
4 tablespoons quick-cooking granulated tapioca
4 large Granny Smith apples, peeled and grated
½ teaspoon ground cinnamon
⅛ teaspoon ground nutmeg
Sliced toasted almonds, for garnish (optional)
Lemon Tofu Crème (page 114), for garnish (optional)

Preheat the oven to 350°F. Lightly oil a 9-inch pie pan with canola oil spray.

Make the crust by mixing the oats, applesauce, and salt. Press into the prepared pie pan and bake for 30 minutes, until lightly golden.

To make the filling, combine the apple juice, agave nectar, and tapioca in a saucepan. Let sit for 5 minutes, then bring to a boil, stirring constantly. Lower the heat and cook until the tapioca thickens and becomes clear. Add the apples and mix well with the cinnamon and nutmeg. Pour into the piecrust and chill until set, about 2 hours.

For a nutty flavor and texture, sprinkle the top of the pie with the almonds. For a real treat, serve with a dollop of lemon tofu crème.

Blueberry Pie with Almond Crumb Topping

SERVES | 12 · ☼ VEGAN

The crumbly cinnamon and almond topping gives this blueberry pie a sweet and crunchy crown. Serve warm with a scoop of vanilla ice cream for a scrumptious dessert that will make you nostalgic for the good old days. Although you'll need only 1 crust for this pie, I'd advise against cutting the piecrust recipe in half since it will make it difficult to handle. Instead, freeze the extra pie dough. You'll be halfway done the next time your urge for pie comes up. Make this pie vegan by using butter substitute in the topping and crust.

1 No-Fail Piecrust, unbaked (page 77)

FILLING

6 cups fresh blueberries, or frozen
    blueberries thawed and drained
½ cup light agave nectar
Juice of 1 lemon
¼ cup arrowroot powder

TOPPING

1 cup sprouted spelt flour or
    whole wheat pastry flour
⅓ cup almond flour (blanched almond meal)
½ teaspoon ground cinnamon
¼ teaspoon sea salt
5 tablespoons unsalted butter or
    nonhydrogenated butter substitute
⅓ cup light agave nectar

Preheat the oven to 350°F.

Mix all the filling ingredients together in a bowl and pour into the unbaked piecrust.

In a separate bowl, mix the topping ingredients with your fingers until blended. Crumble over the pie filling. Place the pie in the oven with a baking sheet on the rack below to catch any juices that spill. Bake for 40 to 50 minutes, until the crumb topping is golden and the filling is bubbly.

All-American Apple Pie

SERVES | 12   ✤ VEGAN

Here's a picture-perfect apple pie—filled mile high with juicy apples. Sprouted spelt flour makes the crust unbelievably flaky and easy to work with. Serve it hot with a generous helping of vanilla ice cream and listen to the raves. For a vegan version, use butter substitute instead of butter, and serve with Soy Vanilla Ice Cream (page 83).

No-Fail Piecrust, unbaked (page 77)
6 large Granny Smith apples, peeled and sliced
3 tablespoons sprouted spelt flour or
    whole wheat pastry flour
2 tablespoons fresh lemon juice
¾ cup light agave nectar
2 teaspoons ground cinnamon
¼ teaspoon ground nutmeg
Pinch of sea salt
1 tablespoon unsalted butter or
    nonhydrogenated butter substitute,
    cut into small pieces

Preheat the oven to 425°F.

In a large bowl, toss together the apples, flour, lemon juice, agave nectar, cinnamon, nutmeg, salt, and butter and mix well. Pour into the unbaked pie crust. Top with the second crust and seal with fluted edges. Cover the edges with small pieces of foil to prevent burning. Using a sharp knife, cut 4 slits in the top of the piecrust to allow steam to escape. Bake for 10 minutes, then lower the temperature to 350°F. Continue baking for 25 to 30 minutes, until the crust turns golden.

Chocolate Almond Silk Pie

SERVES | 8–10 ☼ VEGAN

This is a delectably creamy vegan pie with a deep, rich chocolate almond flavor. I love it topped with soy whipped cream. This dessert will satisfy the most discerning chocoholic—guaranteed.

CRUST

1½ cups sprouted spelt flour
   or whole wheat pastry flour
1 cup raw almonds, ground to a
   fine meal in a food processor
1 teaspoon ground cinnamon
½ teaspoon sea salt
3 tablespoons canola oil
2 tablespoons light agave nectar
3 tablespoons water

FILLING

½ cup unsweetened soy milk
1½ tablespoons agar flakes
4 ounces unsweetened chocolate
1½ pounds firm silken tofu, drained
1 cup light agave nectar
2 teaspoons vanilla extract
2 tablespoons amaretto
½ teaspoon almond extract
Chopped toasted almonds and soy
   whipped cream, for garnish

Preheat the oven to 325°F.

Prepare the piecrust by mixing the flour, almond meal, cinnamon, and salt in a bowl. In a separate bowl, mix the canola oil, agave nectar, and water. Pour the wet mixture over the dry ingredients and mix well. Press into a 9-inch pie pan and make a fluted rim. Bake for 20 to 25 minutes until golden. Let cool and set aside.

To make the filling, place the soy milk and agar flakes in a small saucepan and bring to a simmer over medium-low heat, stirring often. Continue simmering until the agar flakes dissolve. Set aside.

Melt the chocolate over a double boiler or in a glass bowl in the microwave on high for about 2 minutes. Stir well to melt all the chocolate. Place the soy milk mixture, chocolate, tofu, agave nectar, vanilla extract, amaretto, and almond extract in a food processor. Blend together until very smooth and creamy, scraping down the bowl occasionally, about 2 to 3 minutes Spoon the mixture into the cooled piecrust and refrigerate until set and firm, 2 or more hours. Garnish with chopped toasted almonds and soy whipped cream.

Maple Pecan Tart

SERVES | 12

The usual corn syrup is replaced with agave nectar in this elegant tart. It's beautiful on a holiday dessert table or at any get-together.

Oat Pastry Piecrust, prebaked (page 78)
3 tablespoons unsalted butter
¾ cup amber agave nectar
3 large eggs or ¾ cup egg substitute
1 tablespoon bourbon or dark rum
1 teaspoon vanilla extract
1½ teaspoons maple extract
½ teaspoon ground cinnamon
½ cup pecans, coarsely chopped and
    roasted in a 350°F oven for 5 minutes
2 tablespoons sprouted spelt flour
2 cups pecan halves
Sinfully Rich Vanilla Bean Ice Cream (page 82),
    Soy Vanilla Ice Cream (page 83), or
    Agave Nectar Whipped Cream (page 113),
    for garnish (optional)

Preheat the oven to 350°F.

Prepare the pie dough, press into a 10-inch tart pan with a removable bottom, and bake for 5 minutes.

To prepare the filling, beat the butter and agave nectar with an electric mixer until fluffy. Add the eggs, 1 at a time, and beat again until well combined. Add the bourbon, vanilla extract, maple extract, and cinnamon and mix until combined. In a separate bowl, mix the chopped pecans with the flour and fold them into the egg mixture. Pour into the prebaked piecrust and bake for 15 minutes, or until the filling is lightly set.

Remove the tart from the oven and arrange the pecan halves in concentric circles over the top of the tart, pressing down lightly into the filling. Bake for another 30 minutes, or until completely set. Halfway through baking, cover the tart with tented foil to prevent the pecans from overbrowning. Remove from the oven and cool on a cooling rack. Serve warm with vanilla ice cream or whipped cream.

Caramel Macadamia Nut Tart

SERVES | 12

Without a doubt, this is the richest dessert in this cookbook. It's an adapted and revised version of one of my restaurant's most beloved desserts, Walnut Passion Bars. I've turned them into a tart and added buttery macadamias.

CHOCOLATE CRUST

½ cup unsalted butter, melted

⅓ cup light agave nectar

1 large egg

1 teaspoon vanilla extract

Pinch of sea salt

⅓ cup plus 1 tablespoon unsweetened cocoa powder

½ cup sprouted spelt flour or whole wheat pastry flour

FILLING

½ cup unsalted butter

2 cups amber agave nectar

¼ teaspoon sea salt

½ cup light cream

3 cups whole raw macadamia nuts

1 teaspoon vanilla extract

Sinfully Rich Vanilla Bean Ice Cream (page 82) or Agave Nectar Whipped Cream (page 113), for garnish (optional)

Preheat the oven to 325°F. Line the bottom of a 10-inch removable bottom tart pan with a circle of parchment paper.

In an electric mixer, beat together all the crust ingredients until smooth and creamy. Pour the batter into the prepared tart pan and bake for 15 minutes, or until the crust is set.

For the filling, combine the butter, agave nectar, and salt in a saucepan. Bring to a boil. The mixture should reach 250°F on a candy thermometer. Remove from the heat and stir in the cream, nuts, and vanilla extract. Pour into the prebaked crust and return to the oven for 15 to 20 minutes, until golden and bubbly.

Important note: place the tart pan on a baking sheet before placing in the oven. This will prevent the caramel from dripping inside your oven and make it easier to remove the hot tart from the oven.

Cool the tart to room temperature, then refrigerate for 4 or more hours. It will look a bit gooey at first, but the caramel hardens when refrigerated. When the tart has set, carefully cut out wedges, remembering to peel off the parchment paper. This tart is difficult to remove as a whole from the pan because of the hardened caramel topping, so you'll need to cut it into individual pieces to serve. Serve warm with vanilla ice cream or whipped cream.

French Pear Frangipane Tarte

SERVES | 12

While vacationing in Paris, I fell in love with the delicious fruit tarts. Here is my whole grain, sugar-free version with a fragrant frangipane filling made in the classic tradition using finely ground almonds. Now you can indulge and feel great afterwards. *C'est magnifique.*

Sweet Pastry Crust (page 76), pressed
  into a 10-inch tart pan with removable
  bottom and prebaked for 10 minutes

FILLING

4 tablespoons unsalted butter or
  nonhydrogenated butter substitute,
  at room temperature
⅓ cup light agave nectar
2 large eggs
½ cup almond meal
½ teaspoon almond extract
2 tablespoons Kirsch

TOPPING

4 ripe Bartlett pears
2 tablespoons fresh lemon juice
1½ tablespoons light agave nectar
3 tablespoons juice-sweetened apricot jam
Sinfully Rich Vanilla Bean Ice Cream (page 82),
  Soy Vanilla Ice Cream (page 83), or
  Agave Nectar Whipped Cream (page 113),
  for garnish (optional)

Preheat the oven to 325°F.

To make the filling, using an electric mixer, cream the butter and agave nectar together until light and fluffy. Add the eggs and beat again. Add almond meal, almond extract, and Kirsch. Beat well. Pour into the prebaked tart crust.

To make the topping, peel and halve the pears, drizzling with the lemon juice as you go to keep them from turning brown. Slice each pear half into thin slices, keeping them together at the stem end (do not cut through). Fan out the pears slightly and place each over the filling in a circular pattern. Drizzle the agave nectar over the pears and bake for 40 to 45 minutes, or until they turn a light golden brown.

Warm the apricot jam in a saucepan over low heat and brush or drizzle over the pears. Let the tart cool slightly. It's best served warm with vanilla ice cream or whipped cream.

VARIATION

Apricot Frangipane Tart: When in season, substitute fresh ripe apricots for the pears for a special treat. Depending on the size, 8 to 10 apricots should be sufficient to cover a 10-inch tart. Cut the apricots in half and place, cut sides down, over the filling. Bake as directed above.

Fresh Fruit Tart

SERVES | 8

Here you have the Queen of Tarts: fresh figs and apricot jam are a wonderful counterpart to the sweet and tangy taste of the seasonal berries and kiwi.

Vanilla Pastry Cream (page 111)
Sweet Pastry Crust, prebaked in a 10-inch
  removable bottom tart pan (this page)
1 pint strawberries, rinsed, hulled, and halved
½ pint raspberries, rinsed and drained
1 pint blueberries, rinsed and drained
2 or 3 ripe kiwis, peeled and sliced
2 ripe fresh figs, cut into quarters (optional)
⅓ cup juice-sweetened apricot jam
Agave Nectar Whipped Cream (page 113)

Prepare the pastry cream and pour it immediately into the prebaked tart crust. Cover with plastic wrap that rests gently on the surface of the custard to prevent a skin from forming. Refrigerate for 2 hours or more.

Arrange the strawberries, raspberries, blueberries, kiwis, and figs (if using) decoratively and generously over the top of the pastry cream in the tart (you may have some left over). Heat the apricot jam in a small saucepan until melted and syrupy. Brush the apricot glaze over the fruit. Store tart in the refrigerator until ready to serve. Garnish with whipped cream.

Sweet Pastry Crust

MAKES | 2 CRUSTS (9-INCH PIE
OR 10-INCH TART)

This is a perfect crust to use with fillings that will benefit from a hint of extra sweetness. Because this is a fairly durable crust, it's an excellent choice for making bite-size tartlets or other finger-food desserts.

4 tablespoons unsalted butter or
  nonhydrogenated butter substitute,
  at room temperature
2 tablespoons light agave nectar
¼ teaspoon sea salt
3 large egg yolks
1 teaspoon vanilla extract
1½ cups sprouted spelt flour or
  whole wheat pastry flour

In an electric mixer, cream together the butter, agave nectar, and salt until light and fluffy. Add the egg yolks and vanilla extract and beat well. Stir in the flour and mix until just combined but still crumbly. Divide the dough in half and roll out on a lightly floured surface, making a circle a little larger than the pie pan. Place into the pie pan and flute the edges. Refrigerate or freeze the other half of the dough for later use.

Note: For recipes calling for a prebaked piecrust, preheat the oven to 325°F, prick the crust all over with a fork and bake for 12 to 15 minutes, until lightly golden. Cool and fill.

No-Fail Piecrust

MAKES | TWO 9-INCH CRUSTS

✺ VEGAN

The key to this amazingly thin and flaky crust is to freeze the butter (or butter substitute for a vegan version) and chill the flour so both are super-cold. Doing so creates lots of flaky air pockets in the crust. Easy as pie.

1½ cups sprouted spelt flour or
    whole wheat pastry flour, chilled in
    the freezer for about 30 minutes
½ teaspoon sea salt
½ cup frozen unsalted butter or
    nonhydrogenated butter substitute,
    cut into small pieces
5 tablespoons ice water

In a food processor, pulse the flour and salt 5 or 6 times to fluff up the flour with air. Add the butter and pulse until the mixture resembles coarse crumbs. Do not overmix. Add the ice water and process by pulsing until the mixture just starts to stick together (if processed too much, the dough won't be flaky).

Divide the dough in half and flatten slightly into 2 disks. Flour the dough a little and place each disk between 2 pieces of waxed paper. Wrap well with plastic wrap and refrigerate for 1 hour or more, until ready to use. Place 1 disk on a lightly floured surface. Roll the dough into a circle about 2 inches larger than the pie pan. This dough is easy to roll out thinly.

To prevent cracks or tears, lift the dough by rolling it back onto the rolling pin, then roll it over your dish. Gently press the dough into the bottom of the pie pan. Fill the pie with the filling of your choice. Roll the second crust and place over the filling. Press the edges together and flute by pinching the dough together with 2 fingers. Cover the edges of the crust with strips of aluminum foil to prevent the crust from getting too brown. Remove the foil during the last 5 to 10 minutes of baking.

For a prebaked bottom crust, preheat the oven to 350°F. Prick the bottom and sides of the crust with a fork. Bake for about 10 minutes, or until lightly browned. Cool before filling.

Oat Pastry Piecrust

MAKES | ONE 9-INCH CRUST

🌀 VEGAN

Here's a staple no-roll piecrust
that's assembled in minutes.

1½ cups regular rolled oats
   (not quick cooking) ground to a
   fine meal in a food processor
½ cup sprouted spelt flour or
   whole wheat pastry flour
Pinch of salt
¼ cup canola oil
¼ cup light agave nectar
¼ cup water

Lightly oil a 9-inch pie pan with canola oil
spray. Mix the oats, flour, and salt in a
bowl. In a separate bowl, mix the canola
oil, agave nectar, and water. Add the oil
mixture to the flour mixture and stir to
combine. Form a dough and let rest for
10 minutes.

   Press the dough into the prepared pie
pan. Flute the edges of the piecrust
by pinching the dough together with
2 fingers.

   To prebake the piecrust, preheat the oven
to 325°F. Bake for 20 to 25 minutes, until
golden.

Nut Pastry Crust

MAKES | ONE 9-INCH CRUST

🌀 VEGAN

Another no-roll piecrust—
life is good.

1 cup walnuts or pecans, ground to
   a fine meal in a food processor
1 cup oat flour
½ cup barley flour
Pinch of sea salt
½ teaspoon ground cinnamon
3 tablespoons canola oil
2 tablespoons light agave nectar
3 tablespoons water

Lightly oil a 9-inch pie pan with canola oil
spray. Mix the walnut meal, oat flour, barley flour, salt, and cinnamon in a large
bowl. In a small bowl, mix together the
canola oil, agave nectar, and water. Add the
oil mixture to the flour mixture and stir to
combine.

   Press the dough into the prepared pie
pan. Build up the edges of the piecrust and
flute with 2 fingers.

   To prebake the piecrust, preheat the
oven to 325°F. Bake for 20 to 25 minutes,
until golden.

Apple Walnut Crumble

SERVES | 10–12   ❋ VEGAN

This apple crumble is the ultimate healthy-eating comfort food. Together the warm cinnamon apples and the rich walnut topping can't be beat. Combining apples of mixed texture works best. A firm variety such as Golden Delicious will retain its shape and texture while a Cortland will lend itself beautifully to producing a thick, delicious sauce.

FILLING

6 to 7 large apples, peeled and sliced
Juice of 1 lemon
¼ cup light agave nectar
3 tablespoons arrowroot powder
2 teaspoons ground cinnamon
Pinch of ground nutmeg
½ cup cold water

TOPPING

½ cup light agave nectar
2½ teaspoons ground cinnamon
⅓ cup canola oil
1 cup walnuts, ground to a coarse meal
   in a food processor
1 cup walnuts, coarsely chopped
1 cup regular rolled oats (not quick cooking),
   ground to a coarse meal in a food processor
½ cup barley flour

Sinfully Rich Vanilla Bean Ice Cream (page 82),
   Soy Vanilla Ice Cream (page 83), or
   Skinny Vanilla Bean Frozen Yogurt
   (page 83), for garnish (optional)

Preheat the oven to 325°F.

To make the filling, mix together the apples, lemon juice, agave nectar, arrowroot powder, cinnamon, and nutmeg in a large bowl. Spoon the filling into a 9- by 13-inch glass baking pan. Pour the water over the filling to provide extra moisture.

To make the topping, in a bowl whisk together the agave nectar, cinnamon, and canola oil. Mix the ground walnuts, chopped walnuts, rolled oats, and barley flour in a separate bowl. Combine the flour mixture and the oil mixture together and mix with your fingers until blended and crumbly. Crumble the topping evenly over the apple mixture. The topping will be wet and sticky. Bake for 30 to 35 minutes, until the topping is golden and the filling is bubbly.

Serve warm with vanilla ice cream or frozen yogurt.

Summer Berry Peach Cobbler

SERVES | 8–10

Sweet blueberries and juicy peaches remind me of summer. With its buttery biscuit topping, this cobbler brings back memories of backyard picnics and barbeques. Don't forget the ice cream when serving this dessert. If you like, you can substitute the buttermilk with low-fat plain kefir, a cultured yogurtlike drink. Full of *Lactobacillus acidophilus*, a beneficial probiotic that aids in digestion, kefir is widely available at health food stores.

FILLING

4 large ripe peaches, sliced
1 pint fresh blueberries, rinsed
¼ cup light agave nectar
Juice of 1 lemon
½ teaspoon ground cinnamon

TOPPING

1½ cups sprouted spelt flour or
   whole wheat pastry flour
1½ teaspoons baking powder
1 teaspoon baking soda
1 teaspoon sea salt
¼ teaspoon ground cinnamon
2½ tablespoons unsalted butter or
   nonhydrogenated butter substitute,
   very cold

1 teaspoon freshly grated lemon zest
¼ cup light agave nectar
½ cup buttermilk or low-fat plain kefir
Sinfully Rich Vanilla Bean Ice Cream (page 82)
   or Soy Vanilla Ice Cream (page 83),
   for garnish (optional)

Preheat the oven to 375°F.

To make the filling, toss all the filling ingredients together in a bowl. Spoon into an 8-inch square baking pan.

To make the topping, pulse the flour, baking powder, baking soda, salt, and cinnamon in a food processor with the cold butter until it resembles coarse meal. Place the mixture in a bowl. In a separate bowl, whisk together the lemon zest, agave nectar, and buttermilk. Make a well in the center of the flour mixture and slowly pour the buttermilk mixture into the well. Use a fork to gently stir the ingredients together to form a dough. Turn the dough out onto a lightly floured work surface and pat into an 8-inch square. Drape the dough carefully over the fruit, cobbling it by pinching it all over the top. Take care not to tear it. If you do make a hole, just press the dough together with your wet fingers. Prick the dough all over with a fork and bake for 35 to 40 minutes, until golden. Let cool in the pan for 15 to 20 minutes to set before serving. Serve with vanilla ice cream if desired.

Ice Creams, Frozen Yogurts, and Sorbets

Sinfully Rich Vanilla Bean Ice Cream

MAKES | 1 QUART ✸ GLUTEN-FREE

This is the real thing: real vanilla beans and real heavy cream reminiscent of old-time creamery blends. This is better than any store-bought premium brand—and it's sugar-free. Here's a tip: make your ice cream base the day before and refrigerate it overnight. The colder it is when you get ready to freeze, the better it will turn out.

1 cup whole milk
1 vanilla bean, split lengthwise
    and seeds scraped
½ cup light agave nectar
Pinch of sea salt
2 large egg yolks
2 cups heavy cream

Have a large bowl of ice water ready. Place the milk in a small saucepan with the vanilla bean, vanilla seeds, agave nectar, and salt. Heat over low heat until the mixture is hot. Lightly beat the egg yolks in a bowl. Add ¼ cup of the hot milk and whisk. Pour the egg mixture into the saucepan and cook over low heat, stirring constantly until it starts to thicken, about 10 minutes.

Remove from the heat and place the saucepan in a bowl of ice water. Continue stirring to cool down the mixture. When the mixture is only slightly warm, stir in the cream. Remove the vanilla bean and discard. Cover and chill in the refrigerator until cold—several hours or overnight is best. Pour the mixture through a strainer into the ice cream maker and freeze according to the manufacturer's instructions.

VARIATIONS

Be creative. During the last 5 minutes of freezing, add approximately ½ cup of your favorite ice cream mixers. Some suggestions:
Toasted nuts
Grain-sweetened chocolate chips
Chopped dried fruit
Crumbled cookies (made with agave, of course)
Agave brownie crumbles

Soy Vanilla Ice Cream

MAKES | 1 QUART

◈ VEGAN   ◈ GLUTEN-FREE

Here's a nondairy vegan alternative. Delish.

1 cup soy creamer

2 cups unsweetened soy milk

1 vanilla bean, split lengthwise
   and seeds scraped

1½ tablespoons arrowroot powder

½ cup light agave nectar

½ teaspoon xanthan gum

Heat the soy creamer, 1½ cups of the soy milk, the vanilla bean, and vanilla seeds in a saucepan until the mixture comes to a boil. Remove the pan from the heat and allow the vanilla bean to steep in the milk mixture for 20 minutes. While the mixture is cooling, prepare a slurry by mixing together the remaining ½ cup soy milk with the arrowroot powder. Add the agave nectar to the milk mixture and return to a boil. Decrease the heat and whisk in the slurry. Continue whisking until the mixture just begins to thicken. Remove from the heat and whisk in the xanthan gum. Let cool to room temperature, then refrigerate for several hours or overnight until cold. Remove the vanilla bean and freeze in the ice cream maker according to the manufacturer's directions.

Skinny Vanilla Bean Frozen Yogurt

MAKES | 1 QUART   ◈ GLUTEN-FREE

I'm a big vanilla ice cream fan, so I had to create a great-tasting, low-fat alternative to enjoy guilt-free. Use a fresh vanilla bean and thick, Greek-style yogurt for best results.

1 cup (1 percent) low-fat milk

¾ cup light agave nectar

1 vanilla bean, split lengthwise
   and seeds scraped

1 cup nonfat plain Greek-style yogurt

⅓ cup nonfat dry milk

1 teaspoon xanthan gum

Pinch of sea salt

In a small saucepan, combine the milk, agave nectar, vanilla bean, and vanilla seeds. Bring to a simmer, then remove from the heat and let the vanilla bean steep for ½ hour in the milk mixture. Remove the vanilla bean from the cooled milk and reserve. In a food processor, blend together the milk mixture, yogurt, dry milk, xanthan gum, and salt until smooth and creamy, about 1 minute. Pour into a container, replace the vanilla bean, and allow it to infuse the mixture for several hours or overnight. When ready to freeze, discard the vanilla bean and freeze in the ice cream maker according to the manufacturer's directions.

Strawberry Ice Cream

MAKES | 1½ QUARTS ⚙ GLUTEN-FREE

This strawberry ice cream has an old-fashioned pale pink color with delicious chunks of whole fruit inside. Using light cream and milk in place of heavy cream reduces the fat and calories without compromising the taste.

2 cups ripe strawberries, sliced
¾ cup light agave nectar
1 cup whole milk
¼ teaspoon sea salt
1½ cups light cream
1 tablespoon vanilla extract
1 teaspoon xanthan gum

In a food processor, combine 1 cup of the strawberries with the agave nectar, milk, salt, cream, vanilla extract, and xanthan gum. Blend until smooth, approximately 1 to 2 minutes. Add the remaining 1 cup strawberries and pulse 5 to 6 times, leaving some larger pieces of strawberries. Refrigerate for several hours or overnight until ready to freeze. Pour into the ice cream maker and follow the manufacturer's instructions for freezing.

Chocolate Tofu Ice Cream

MAKES | 1 QUART ⚙ VEGAN

To achieve a rich chocolate taste, use a high-quality cocoa powder.

16 ounces soft silken tofu
   (refrigerated variety)
½ cup unsweetened soy milk
3 tablespoons canola oil
¾ cup light agave nectar
¼ cup unsweetened cocoa powder
1 tablespoon vanilla extract
Pinch of sea salt

Combine the tofu, soy milk, canola oil, agave nectar, cocoa powder, vanilla extract, and salt in a food processor and blend until creamy, about 2 to 3 minutes. Refrigerate several hours or overnight until ready to freeze. Pour into the ice cream maker and follow the manufacturer's instructions for freezing.

Chocolate Gelato

MAKES | 1 QUART ☀ GLUTEN-FREE

The small amount of coffee substitute used will enhance the intensity of the chocolate but will not impart a mocha flavor. This is a creamy, decadent chocolate treat.

1 teaspoon unflavored gelatin
¼ cup cold water
3 ounces unsweetened chocolate
1½ cups (1 percent) low-fat milk
1½ cups heavy cream
1 tablespoon natural coffee substitute or instant coffee
½ cup light agave nectar
1 teaspoon vanilla extract
Pinch of sea salt

Have a large bowl of ice water ready. Soften the gelatin in the ¼ cup cold water. Melt the chocolate over a double boiler or in a glass plate in the microwave on high setting for about 1½ minutes. Stir well to melt all the chocolate. In a heavy saucepan, heat the milk and ½ cup of the cream. When the mixture is hot, but not boiling, add the coffee substitute, agave nectar, and gelatin. Whisk well, until the gelatin is dissolved completely. Remove from the heat and whisk in the chocolate, vanilla extract, and salt.

Pour the mixture into a bowl and set it into the bowl of ice water to accelerate cooling. Cover and refrigerate until ready to freeze. Right before freezing, whip the remaining 1 cup heavy cream until soft peaks form. Gently fold into the chocolate mixture. Refrigerate for several hours or overnight, until cold. Pour into the ice cream maker and follow the manufacturer's instructions for freezing.

Watermelon Sorbet

MAKES | 1 QUART

⚛ VEGAN   ⚛ GLUTEN-FREE

This particular sorbet is like really good Italian ice. It's got an icier texture than some of the other sorbet recipes because it's made from fruit that has a naturally high water content. It's most appealing and quite refreshing on a hot summer day.

Half of a small seedless watermelon,
   rind removed, cut into pieces
½ cup light agave nectar
2 tablespoons fresh lime juice
Pinch of sea salt

Place the watermelon pieces in a food processor and blend until liquefied, about 1 to 2 minutes. Measure out 3 cups of the watermelon purée into a large bowl. Add the agave nectar, lime juice, and salt and combine well. Refrigerate for several hours or overnight until ready to freeze. Pour into the ice cream maker and follow the manufacturer's instructions for freezing. Freeze 20 minutes. Transfer to a plastic storage container and place in a regular home freezer to firm up. Remove the sorbet from the freezer 10 minutes before serving to allow time to soften up.

Raspberry Sorbet

MAKES | 1 QUART

⚛ VEGAN   ⚛ GLUTEN-FREE

This is a must-have in the Catalano home. The flavor of this sorbet is intense, and the color is gorgeous. This versatile dessert is a light, refreshing way to end any meal. Melted, it makes a delicious complement to vanilla ice cream or scrumptious sauce for chocolate cake.

24 ounces unsweetened
   frozen raspberries, thawed
1 cup light agave nectar
⅔ cup water
1 tablespoon fresh lemon juice

Blend the raspberries in a food processor until puréed, about 1 minute. Pour into a large bowl and add the agave nectar, water, and lemon juice. Strain the mixture through a sieve, using a rubber spatula to help push the purée through. Discard the seeds. Refrigerate for several hours or overnight until ready to freeze. Pour into the ice cream maker and follow the manufacturer's instructions for freezing.

Toasted Almond Amaretto Ice Cream

This ice cream is fabulous drizzled with hot fudge sauce—a decidedly sophisticated treat for adults.

2 cups half-and-half

1 cup (2 percent) reduced fat milk

⅓ cup nonfat dry milk

½ cup pasteurized egg substitute

½ cup amber agave nectar

1 teaspoon vanilla extract

2 tablespoons amaretto, or

  ⅛ teaspoon almond extract

Pinch of sea salt

½ cup lightly toasted almonds,

  coarsely chopped

Hot Fudge Sauce (page 107) (optional)

Place the half-and-half, milk, dry milk, egg substitute, agave nectar, vanilla extract, amaretto, and salt in a food processor and blend until well combined, about 1 minute. Refrigerate for several hours or overnight. Blend the mixture again, then pour into the ice cream maker and freeze according to the manufacturer's directions. Add the toasted almonds 5 minutes before the ice cream is ready. Serve with hot fudge sauce, if desired.

Pistachio Ice Cream

Let the others turn green with envy. This pistachio ice cream is a reduced-fat version, but has all the taste and texture of the classic.

1 cup half-and-half

2 cups (2 percent) reduced fat milk

½ cup pasteurized egg substitute

½ cup light agave nectar

2 teaspoons vanilla extract

⅛ teaspoon almond extract

Pinch of sea salt

¼ teaspoon guar gum

¼ teaspoon xanthan gum

½ cup shelled, roasted, unsalted

  pistachio nuts (natural shell)

Place the half-and-half, milk, egg substitute, agave nectar, vanilla extract, almond extract, salt, guar gum, and xanthan gum in a food processor and blend until well combined, about 1 minute. Refrigerate several hours or overnight until ready to freeze. Blend the mixture again, then pour into the ice cream maker and freeze according to the manufacturer's directions. Add the pistachios 5 minutes before the ice cream is ready.

Special Treats

Tropical Rice Pudding

SERVES | 4–6

✸ VEGAN   ✸ GLUTEN-FREE

This is a simple, yet totally memorable, way to serve rice pudding as a special dessert. The coconut cream and tropical fruits make a perfect ending to a Latin- or Island-themed menu. You can find sweet brown rice at natural food stores.

1 cup sweet brown rice
2 cups cold water
Pinch of sea salt
2 (14-ounce) cans unsweetened
 coconut milk (not light)
½ cup light agave nectar
1 teaspoon vanilla extract
1 mango, sliced
1 banana, sliced
6 slices pineapple
Lightly toasted unsweetened
 coconut, for garnish

Place rice, water, and salt in a heavy saucepan and bring to a boil. Decrease the heat and cook covered over low heat for 40 minutes. Do not uncover until the rice is done. Remove from the heat and uncover.

Stir 1 can of coconut milk and the agave nectar into the rice and bring to a boil. Decrease the heat to a simmer and cook, stirring frequently, about 5 minutes, or until thickened. Remove from the heat and stir in the vanilla extract. Let cool to room temperature, then refrigerate. Skim the cream off the top of the second can of coconut milk and set aside. (Use the rest of the coconut milk for another purpose.) To serve, spoon the rice pudding onto individual plates or into bowls. Arrange the mango, banana, and pineapple slices around the pudding and drizzle coconut cream on top. Sprinkle with toasted coconut and serve.

Compote of Pears in Spiced Port

SERVES | 6

✿ VEGAN   ✿ GLUTEN-FREE

In this light and elegant dessert, the pears turn a beautiful rosy color from the wine. The slightly tart taste of lemon topping drizzled over the pears and the crunch of toasted pistachios complete the dish.

½ cup light agave nectar
½ cup ruby port
1 cinnamon stick
1 vanilla bean, split in half lengthwise
2 long strips of lemon rind
6 cups water
6 ripe but firm pears such as Bartlett or Anjou, peeled and cut in half lengthwise
Lemon Tofu Crème (page 114) (optional)
½ cup lightly toasted pistachios or hazelnuts, chopped, for garnish

In a large pot, combine the agave nectar, port, cinnamon, vanilla bean, lemon rind, and water. Bring to a boil. Add the pears, decrease the heat to a simmer, and cook uncovered for about 10 minutes, or until the pears are tender when pierced with a fork.

Remove the pears from the cooking liquid with a slotted spoon and set aside. Continue to simmer the liquid for about 5 minutes, or until reduced to about 1½ cups and of a syrupy consistency.

Serve the pears either warm or cold with some port sauce and a drizzle of lemon tofu crème. Sprinkle with toasted pistachios.

Grilled Peaches with Caramelized Brandy Pecan Sauce

SERVES | 4

✹ VEGAN   ✹ GLUTEN-FREE

Warm fruit desserts with ice cream are definitely satisfying. This one, with a delectable brandied pecan sauce, is a real winner. My friend (and fellow gourmand) Edward Eglowsky says he could have these peaches for breakfast, lunch, and dinner. Here's the recipe, Ed.

PECAN SAUCE

3 tablespoons unsalted butter or nonhydrogenated butter substitute
¾ cup pecan halves
⅓ cup amber agave nectar
3 tablespoons heavy cream or soy creamer
2 tablespoons brandy
1 tablespoon amaretto (optional)
¼ teaspoon freshly grated nutmeg

PEACHES

2 tablespoons unsalted butter or nonhydrogenated butter substitute, melted
2 teaspoons ground cinnamon
4 large ripe but firm peaches, cut in half and pitted

Sinfully Rich Vanilla Bean Ice Cream (page 82), Soy Vanilla Ice Cream (page 83), or Skinny Vanilla Bean Frozen Yogurt (page 83)

Prepare the sauce by melting the butter in a saucepan. Add the pecans and sauté over medium heat for about 3 to 4 minutes, until lightly toasted and fragrant.

Add the agave nectar, cream, brandy, amaretto (if using), and nutmeg. Stir and simmer until just slightly thickened, 1 to 2 minutes. If necessary, the sauce can be reheated prior to serving.

To grill the peaches, preheat the grill or grill pan. Make sure your grill is very clean and hot. Mix the butter and cinnamon together in a bowl. Brush each peach half on both sides with a bit of the melted butter mixture. Grill the peaches with cut-side down first, until slightly scorched by the grill on each side. Do not overcook or they will be mushy.

To serve, place 2 peach halves on each serving plate and spoon some hot pecan sauce over them. Serve with a scoop of vanilla ice cream or frozen yogurt.

Bananas Flambé over Crêpes

SERVES | 4–6

Is there anything more impressive and exciting than a flaming dessert? It's not nearly as complicated as you might imagine, and what better way to make your guests feel special? You can make these crêpes in advance. Refrigerate them for up to 5 days or freeze them with waxed paper between each crêpe. Just bring the crêpes to room temperature and warm on a baking sheet in a 350°F oven for 5 minutes before serving.

CRÊPES

½ cup sprouted spelt flour or
    whole wheat pastry flour
Pinch of sea salt
2 large eggs
1 large egg yolk
1¼ cups (1 percent) low-fat milk or
    unsweetened soy milk
1 teaspoon vanilla extract
2 tablespoons unsalted butter or
    nonhydrogenated butter substitute

BANANAS

3 tablespoons unsalted butter or
    nonhydrogenated butter substitute
½ cup amber agave nectar
Pinch of sea salt
4 ripe but firm large bananas, sliced
½ cup medium or dark rum
½ teaspoon vanilla extract
Sinfully Rich Vanilla Bean Ice Cream (page 82),
    Soy Vanilla Ice Cream (page 83), or Skinny
    Vanilla Bean Frozen Yogurt (page 83)

To prepare the crêpes, sift the flour and salt into a bowl. Whisk in the eggs, egg yolk, and 1 tablespoon of the milk and mix to form a smooth batter. Add the remaining milk and the vanilla extract, whisking until no lumps remain. Let the batter rest at room temperature for 20 to 30 minutes.

To cook the crêpes, use a nonstick 8-inch skillet over medium heat. Melt a small dab (½ teaspoon) of the butter and quickly pour in ¼ cup of the batter, swirling the batter over the entire pan until it covers the pan evenly. Cook for about 1 to 2 minutes, until the edges look dry. Carefully lift and turn the crêpe using a spatula and your fingers to help guide the spatula under the crêpe. Gently flip it over and cook the other side for 30 to 40 seconds, shaking the pan occasionally to release it. Slide the crêpe out of the skillet onto a plate. Repeat this process, making 9 more crêpes, until all the crêpes are cooked and stacked on each other on the plate. Cover to keep warm. >

Prepare the flambé by melting the butter in a large skillet over medium heat. Add the agave nectar and salt and cook until bubbling and slightly thickened. Add the bananas and cook over low to medium heat for 2 to 4 minutes, until the bananas are softened. Add the rum to the pan and carefully ignite the alcohol using a lighter with a long neck. Stir the bananas gently, remove from the heat, and add the vanilla extract.

Fold the warm crêpes into triangles by folding in half twice. For each person, place 2 crêpes on a serving plate and spoon some bananas and sauce over the crêpes. Serve with vanilla ice cream or vanilla frozen yogurt.

Agave Margarita

MAKES | 1 MARGARITA

🌞 VEGAN 🌞 GLUTEN-FREE

Tequila and agave nectar come from the same place: the agave plant. This fun sweet and tart drink reunites them.

Sea salt
Lime wedge
1 ounce light agave nectar
2 ounces freshly squeezed lime juice
3 ounces tequila (blanco, reposado, or añejo)
Orange twist, for garnish

Have ready a chilled, frosted martini glass, a plate of sea salt, and a cocktail shaker with ice. Rub the rim of the cocktail glass with a lime wedge and dip into the sea salt. Pour the agave nectar, lime juice, and tequila into the cocktail shaker with ice. Shake vigorously until very cold. Strain into the prepared glass and serve with a twist of orange.

Frozen Margarita Pie

SERVES | 12

If you want to wow your guests at your next Mexican fiesta, make this dessert. Period. This lime confection is a cross between an ice cream and a pie, and the pretzel crust adds just the right amount of saltiness to make it fun and totally unforgettable.

CRUST

1½ cups whole grain pretzel sticks
¼ cup unsalted butter, melted
⅓ cup light agave nectar

FILLING

1 (12-ounce) can evaporated skim milk
1 tablespoon arrowroot powder
½ cup light agave nectar
Freshly grated zest of 1 lime
6 tablespoons freshly squeezed lime juice
    (about 4 large limes)
2 tablespoons freshly squeezed
    orange juice (about 1 orange)
2 tablespoons good quality,
    preferably aged, tequila
1 tablespoon Cointreau or Triple Sec
½ teaspoon vanilla extract

1 cup heavy cream
Agave Nectar Whipped Cream (page 113)
Lime slices, for garnish

Preheat the oven to 350°F. Lightly oil a 9-inch pie pan with canola oil spray.

To prepare the crust, grind the pretzels to a fine meal in a food processor. Add the butter and agave nectar and pulse to combine. Press into the prepared pie pan to form the crust. Bake for 5 to 7 minutes, until the edges turn slightly golden. Cool before filling.

To make the filling, first prepare an ice water bath. Then make a slurry by mixing 2 tablespoons of the evaporated skim milk and the arrowroot powder together. In a small saucepan, heat the remaining evaporated milk and the agave nectar until the mixture comes to a gentle simmer. Whisk the arrowroot slurry into the saucepan. Stirring constantly, let the mixture thicken slightly. Remove from the heat and place the saucepan in the ice water bath to cool down quickly, whisking often.

Pour the cooled filling mixture into a large bowl and add the lime zest, lime juice, orange juice, tequila, Cointreau, and vanilla extract. Whisk together well. Place in the refrigerator to cool about 30 minutes, or until semifirm.

Whip the cream until soft peaks form. Fold the whipped cream into the cooled lime mixture. Spoon the filling into the pie crust and freeze for about 4 hours, or until firm. To serve, let the pie defrost for about 10 minutes before slicing. Top the pie with lots of whipped cream and garnish with lime slices.

Chocolate Soufflé

SERVES | 6

Looking for a seriously over-the-top chocolate dessert that is very low fat with an unbelievably rich texture and intense chocolate flavor? Who isn't? The cool crème anglaise served over warm, creamy soufflé is a total treat.

⅓ cup half-and-half
3 ounces premium-quality
    unsweetened chocolate, chopped
½ cup unsweetened cocoa powder
⅓ cup water
½ cup amber agave nectar
2 teaspoons vanilla extract
8 large egg whites
Vanilla Crème Anglaise (page 106)
Agave Nectar Whipped Cream (page 113)

Preheat the oven to 375°F. Lightly brush 6 (12-ounce) individual soufflé ramekins with melted butter.

Pour the half-and-half into a saucepan and cook over medium heat until small bubbles appear around the edge and the liquid is just beginning to tremble. Immediately remove from the heat and add the chopped chocolate. Stir well to melt all the chocolate. Make a double boiler by setting a large bowl over a saucepan half filled with boiling water. Place the melted chocolate mixture in the bowl, add the cocoa powder, water, and ¼ cup of the agave nectar. Whisk together well. When the mixture becomes hot, remove from the heat and stir in the vanilla extract.

Make a meringue by beating the egg whites in a large bowl with an electric mixer on medium speed until foamy, about 1 minute. Increase the speed to medium-high and add the remaining ¼ cup agave nectar in a slow, steady stream until the egg whites are stiff and glossy but not dry, another 1 to 2 minutes. Fold half the meringue into the warm chocolate mixture using a large rubber spatula. Then gently fold the chocolate mixture into the remaining meringue.

Spoon the batter into the prepared ramekins. Place on the center rack of the oven with room to rise (you may have to remove the upper rack in the oven). Bake for about 15 minutes, or until puffed. Remove from the oven and serve immediately. Crack the crown with a spoon and drizzle crème anglaise inside. Cap off with a little whipped cream on top.

Individual Orange Soufflés with Grand Marnier Crème Anglaise

SERVES | 6

Soufflés bring to mind fancy French restaurants, special occasions, and loads of calories. Why wait for a special occasion when you can whip up these incredibly light and delicate soufflés at home and save tons of calories? The Grand Marnier sauce is a must. For a richer sauce, you can use a half cup of evaporated skim milk and an equal amount of heavy cream.

CRÈME ANGLAISE

3¾ cups evaporated skim milk
¼ cup heavy cream
3 tablespoons light agave nectar
½ tablespoon arrowroot powder
    mixed with 1 tablespoon cold water
3 tablespoons Grand Marnier
½ teaspoon vanilla extract

SOUFFLÉS

3 tablespoons unsalted butter
¼ cup sprouted spelt flour or
    whole wheat pastry flour
Pinch of sea salt
½ cup (1 percent) low-fat milk
1 teaspoon freshly grated orange zest
⅓ cup freshly squeezed orange juice
    (about 1 orange)
⅓ tablespoon Grand Marnier liqueur (optional)
4 large eggs, separated
⅓ cup light agave nectar
Agave Nectar Whipped Cream (page 113),
    for garnish (optional)

Prepare the crème anglaise in advance. It can be stored for several days in the refrigerator. Place the milk, cream, and agave nectar in a small saucepan over medium heat. Bring to a boil. Decrease the heat.

Add the arrowroot powder slurry to the milk mixture, whisking constantly. Bring the mixture back to a simmer and remove from the heat immediately after the mixture thickens. Stir in the Grand Marnier and vanilla extract. Cool to room temperature and store in the refrigerator. >

> Individual Orange Soufflés with
Grand Marnier Crème Anglaise
(recipe continues)

Begin preparing the soufflés. Preheat the oven to 325°F. Lightly oil 6 (12-ounce) soufflé ramekins with canola oil spray.

In a saucepan, melt the butter over medium heat. Stir in the flour and salt. Add the milk and cook until thick and bubbly, stirring constantly. Remove from the heat. Stir in the orange zest, orange juice, and Grand Marnier. Blend well.

Using an electric mixer, beat the egg yolks until thick and lemon colored. Gradually add the orange mixture and blend well.

In a clean bowl, using clean beaters, beat the egg whites on medium speed until soft peaks form, about 1 to 2 minutes. Gradually drizzle in the agave nectar and beat until stiff glossy peaks form, another 1 to 2 minutes. Do not overbeat or the egg whites will dry. Fold the orange mixture into the egg whites. Spoon into the ramekins and bake for 20 to 25 minutes, until puffed and golden. Serve immediately.

Place a hot soufflé on a plate in front of each guest. Poke a hole in the center of the soufflé with a spoon and spread slightly open. Pour the crème anglaise generously into the opening of the soufflé and over the top. A dollop of whipped cream makes a nice finishing touch.

Light Chocolate Mousse

SERVES | 6–8　🔆 GLUTEN-FREE

This light version of an old favorite tastes like the real deal, only better—no sugar.

6 ounces unsweetened chocolate
12 ounces light firm silken tofu
⅔ cup light agave nectar
2 teaspoons vanilla extract
3 large egg whites
¼ teaspoon sea salt
Fresh raspberries, for garnish (optional)

Melt the chocolate over a double boiler or in a glass plate in the microwave on high setting for about 2 minutes. Stir well to melt all the chocolate. Place the tofu, chocolate, ⅓ cup of the agave nectar, and the vanilla extract in a food processor. Blend until very smooth and there are no pieces of tofu left. This will take several minutes.

Using an electric mixer, beat the egg whites with the salt at medium speed until soft peaks form, about 1 to 2 minutes. Bring the remaining ⅓ cup agave nectar to a rolling boil in a small saucepan. Slowly pour the hot agave nectar syrup into the egg whites and beat on high speed until stiff and glossy, but not dry. Gently fold a quarter of the meringue into the tofu mixture, then fold in the rest until no whites are visible.

Spoon into individual 8-ounce glasses or cups and chill for 3 hours or more. The mousse is delicious garnished with fresh raspberries.

Prune Armagnac Truffles

MAKES | 2 DOZEN ✷ GLUTEN-FREE

This is an all-time favorite recipe from
[...]g classes. A trip to Paris
[...]e to experiment more with
[...]nd chocolate seemed like
[...]t pairing. I think a good
[...]n could do a world of good
[...]s! In spite of their somewhat
[...]putation, prunes have a
[...]ated taste that makes them
[...]sting recipe ingredient.

1 cup unsulfured pitted prunes,
   coarsely chopped
2 tablespoons Armagnac or other brandy
¼ cup heavy cream
½ cup plus 3 tablespoons light agave nectar
3 tablespoons unsalted butter
¼ teaspoon freshly grated nutmeg
6 ounces unsweetened chocolate, chopped
1 tablespoon vanilla extract
1½ cups toasted walnuts, finely chopped

Line a baking sheet with parchment paper
or waxed paper. In a small bowl, combine
the prunes with the Armagnac and set
aside to steep.

In a saucepan, bring the cream, agave
nectar, butter, and nutmeg to a boil.
Remove from the heat and stir in the chocolate and vanilla extract. Whisk until completely melted and smooth. Stir in the
prunes and Armagnac. Freeze the mixture
for 20 minutes, or refrigerate for 1 hour,
until firm enough to mound onto a spoon.
Take a heaping tablespoon of the mixture
and roll it into a ball with the palms of your
hands, then roll it in the walnuts to coat.
Place on the prepared baking sheet and
chill to firm.

Remove the truffles from the refrigerator
10 to 15 minutes prior to serving. Store
them in the refrigerator in an airtight container for up to 2 weeks.

Hazelnut Truffles

MAKES | 20 TRUFFLES

Chocolate lovers, rejoice! Finally, a gourmet chocolate truffle that's sugar-free and not artificially sweetened. These are so easy to make, you may never buy store-bought chocolate again. For a plain, unadulterated chocolate truffle, omit the hazelnut extract and roll the truffles in premium-quality unsweetened cocoa powder. For vegan truffles, substitute soy creamer for the heavy cream, butter substitute for real butter, and instant soy milk powder for the nonfat dry milk.

6 tablespoons heavy cream
⅔ cup light agave nectar
3 tablespoons unsalted butter
6 ounces premium-quality unsweetened
    chocolate, chopped
2 teaspoons vanilla extract
1 teaspoon hazelnut extract
¼ cup nonfat dry milk
1 cup lightly toasted hazelnuts, skinned and
    finely chopped in a food processor

In a saucepan over medium heat, bring the cream, agave nectar, and butter to a boil. Remove from the heat and stir in the chocolate. Whisk until all the chocolate is melted and the mixture is smooth. Stir in the vanilla extract, hazelnut extract, and dry milk. Whisk until smooth. Freeze the mixture for about 20 minutes, or refrigerate for 2 hours, or until firm.

To form a truffle, take a heaping tablespoon of the mixture and roll it into a ball with the palms of your hands. Repeat until all the mixture is used. Roll the truffles in the hazelnuts to coat. Refrigerate to keep firm. Remove the truffles 10 to 15 minutes prior to serving for best taste and texture.

Frostings, Fillings, and Sauces

Vanilla Buttercream Frosting

MAKES | 2 CUPS (FROSTS ONE
9-INCH LAYER CAKE)

🌞 GLUTEN-FREE

This is my favorite frosting. It's a
real buttercream, rich and creamy,
but not too sweet. It's great on
any cake or cupcake.

½ cup unsalted butter, at room temperature
6 tablespoons light agave nectar
1 cup nonfat dry milk
1½ teaspoons vanilla extract
4 tablespoons whole milk
Pinch of sea salt

Cream the butter with an electric mixer
until light in color. Slowly add the agave
nectar and beat until fluffy, about 1 to
2 minutes. Gradually add the dry milk and
beat again. Add the vanilla extract and
the milk, one tablespoon at a time, until
completely blended. Add the salt, turn
the mixer to high speed, and beat about
2 minutes, or until very fluffy. Store in the
refrigerator for up to 3 weeks.

Vanilla Crème Anglaise

MAKES | 1½ CUPS   🌞 GLUTEN-FREE

Substituting evaporated skim
milk for some of the cream reduces
the fat yet maintains the richness
of this classic dessert sauce.

½ cup evaporated skim milk
½ cup heavy cream
1 vanilla bean, split lengthwise
    and seeds scraped
¼ cup light agave nectar
½ teaspoon arrowroot powder
    dissolved in 1 tablespoon cold water

Place the milk, cream, vanilla bean, and
vanilla seeds in a saucepan over medium
heat. Bring to a simmer. Remove from
the heat and let steep for about 15 to
20 minutes.

Add the agave nectar to the milk mixture and bring back to a simmer. Decrease
the heat and add the arrowroot powder
slurry into the milk mixture, whisking
constantly. Bring the mixture back to a
simmer and remove from the heat immediately after it starts to thicken (this happens quickly). Remove the vanilla bean
and cool the sauce to room temperature.
Store in the refrigerator for up to 1 week.
Serve chilled.

Fat-Free Vanilla Yogurt Frosting

MAKES | 2 CUPS (FROSTS ONE 9-INCH LAYER CAKE)

❂ GLUTEN-FREE

The delicately tangy flavor makes a lovely frosting for carrot and banana cakes.

1½ cups plain nonfat Greek-style yogurt
½ cup light agave nectar
6 tablespoons nonfat dry milk
1 tablespoon vanilla extract
Pinch of sea salt

In a food processor, blend together the yogurt, agave nectar, dry milk, vanilla extract, and salt until smooth and creamy, about 1 minute. Refrigerate for 1 to 2 hours to thicken. Whip with an electric mixer to soften and fluff up for a lighter texture.

VARIATIONS

Citrus Crème Frosting: Substitute 3 tablespoons frozen orange juice concentrate for part of the agave nectar, and substitute ½ teaspoon orange extract for the vanilla extract.
Chocolate Frosting: Substitute 3 tablespoons unsweetened cocoa powder for part of the nonfat dry milk. Add extra cocoa for a richer chocolate taste.
Almond Frosting: Decrease the vanilla extract to ½ tablespoon and add ½ teaspoon almond extract. Top the frosting with toasted sliced almonds.

Hot Fudge Sauce

MAKES | 1½ CUPS

❂ VEGAN   ❂ GLUTEN-FREE

For an agave nectar dessert home run, top an Ultimate Fudgy Brownie (page 37) with your choice of vanilla ice cream or frozen yogurt, add this hot fudge sauce, and top it off with Agave Nectar Whipped Cream (page 113).

¾ cup light agave nectar
¼ cup water
¼ cup unsweetened cocoa powder
2 ounces unsweetened chocolate, chopped
2 tablespoons unsalted butter or
    nonhydrogenated butter substitute
⅓ cup heavy cream or soy creamer
1 teaspoon vanilla extract

In a small saucepan, bring the agave nectar to a boil. Decrease heat to medium and simmer for 2 minutes. Stir in the water. Return to a boil and add the cocoa powder. Decrease the heat to low and simmer for 1 minute, stirring constantly. Add the unsweetened chocolate, butter, and cream and bring back to a boil. Remove the mixture from the heat and stir in the vanilla extract. This sauce can be refrigerated for up to 2 weeks. To serve, warm in a saucepan over low heat, or microwave on medium setting for 1 minute. Stir well and serve.

Dark Chocolate Ganache Frosting

MAKES | ABOUT 2 CUPS

☼ GLUTEN-FREE

If you would like to use this ganache as a filling as well as a frosting, double the recipe. You'll have some left over.

8 ounces unsweetened chocolate, chopped
1 cup light agave nectar
¾ cup heavy cream
1 tablespoon unsalted butter
1 tablespoon vanilla extract

Combine the chocolate, agave nectar, and cream in a saucepan. Heat over medium heat until the chocolate melts, stirring constantly. Stir in the butter and vanilla extract. To spread easily, the ganache should be slightly warm, and the consistency of hot fudge.

Vegan Chocolate Ganache Frosting

MAKES | ABOUT 2 CUPS

☼ VEGAN   ☼ GLUTEN-FREE

A few tweaks on Dark Chocolate Ganache Frosting make an equally luscious vegan version. Double this recipe if you want to fill as well as frost a cake (you'll have some left over).

8 ounces unsweetened chocolate, chopped
1 cup light agave nectar
¾ cup nondairy creamer
1 tablespoon nonhydrogenated butter substitute
1 tablespoon vanilla extract

Combine the chocolate, agave nectar, and creamer in a saucepan. Heat over medium heat until the chocolate melts, stirring constantly. Remove from the heat and stir in the butter substitute and vanilla extract. To spread easily, the ganache should be slightly warm, and the consistency of hot fudge.

Milk Chocolate Frosting

MAKES | 2 CUPS (FROSTS ONE
9-INCH LAYER CAKE)

🌞 GLUTEN-FREE

Here's a light and fluffy buttercream frosting for those who like their chocolate pure and simple.

4 ounces unsweetened chocolate, chopped
3 tablespoons unsalted butter
½ cup whole milk
2 teaspoons vanilla extract
½ cup light agave nectar
Pinch of sea salt
1⅓ cups nonfat dry milk

Melt the chocolate and butter in a glass bowl in the microwave for 1½ to 2 minutes. Stir to melt the chocolate completely. Whisk in the milk, vanilla extract, agave nectar, and salt. Blend well. Add the dry milk and whisk until well combined, with no lumps and a spreadable consistency. Cool in the refrigerator for ½ to 1 hour to thicken, then whip with an electric mixer to soften and fluff for a lighter texture.

Vegan Chocolate Buttercream Frosting

MAKES | 2 CUPS (FROSTS ONE
9-INCH LAYER CAKE)

🌞 VEGAN   🌞 GLUTEN-FREE

After a couple of days in the fridge, it may be necessary to whip this frosting with a little soy milk if the consistency is too thick. This will restore a creamy texture.

½ cup nonhydrogenated butter substitute,
    at room temperature
½ cup unsweetened cocoa powder
1 cup light agave nectar
⅓ cup soy milk powder
1 tablespoon vanilla extract

Beat the butter substitute until softened and fluffy. Add the cocoa powder and agave nectar and beat again. Add the soy milk powder, a little at a time, to achieve desired consistency. Add the vanilla extract and beat on high speed until smooth and fluffy. Store in the refrigerator for up to 2 weeks.

Vegan Cream Cheese Frosting

MAKES | 2 CUPS (FROSTS ONE
9-INCH LAYER CAKE)

VEGAN   GLUTEN-FREE

Like traditional cream cheese frosting, this vegan version is a wonderful
compliment to any spiced cake or
cupcake. Spread this frosting
on the vegan Gingerbread Cake
(page 56)—scrumptious!

12 ounces soy cream cheese,
    at room temperature
6 tablespoons nonhydrogenated butter
    substitute, at room temperature
¾ cup light agave nectar
½ tablespoon vanilla extract
Juice of ½ lemon

Using an electric mixer, cream together
the cream cheese and butter substitute.
Add the agave nectar, vanilla extract, and
lemon juice. Beat well until smooth
and fluffy.

Cream Cheese Frosting

MAKES | 2 CUPS (FROSTS ONE
9-INCH LAYER CAKE)

GLUTEN-FREE

I try to cut fat and calories wherever
I can, so I generally use a combination of cream cheese and Neufchâtel
when I prepare this frosting. It's
great on virtually any cake and a
perfect match for Sunrise Carrot
Muffins (page 7).

6 tablespoons unsalted butter,
    at room temperature
12 ounces cream cheese, low-fat Neufchâtel
    cheese, or a combination of both
¾ cup light agave nectar
½ tablespoon vanilla extract
Juice of ½ lemon

Using an electric mixer, cream together
the butter and cream cheese. Add the agave
nectar, vanilla extract, and lemon juice.
Beat well until smooth and fluffy.

VARIATION
Rum Cream Cheese Frosting: Substitute
amber agave nectar for the light agave
nectar and add 1 tablespoon dark rum.

Vanilla Pastry Cream

MAKES | 2 CUPS ☸ GLUTEN-FREE

This is the most versatile filling for many classic desserts. Using a fresh vanilla bean is the key to a great pastry cream.

2 cups whole milk
1 vanilla bean, split lengthwise
   and seeds scraped
4 large egg yolks
¾ cup light agave nectar
¼ cup arrowroot powder
Pinch of sea salt

Place 1½ cups of the milk, the vanilla bean, and vanilla seeds into a saucepan. Bring to a boil. Remove from the heat and let the vanilla bean steep in the hot milk for 15 to 20 minutes. Meanwhile, in a large bowl whisk the egg yolks until creamy. Add the agave nectar to the hot milk and bring to a simmer again over medium heat. Decrease the heat to low. Combine the arrowroot powder, salt, and the remaining ½ cup milk until the powder is completely dissolved.

Temper the egg yolks by whisking in about ½ cup of the hot milk. Working quickly, pour the egg/milk mixture back into the hot milk in the saucepan over low heat and whisk together, stirring constantly, until the mixture is almost at a simmer.

Pour the arrowroot powder slurry into the pan and stir constantly until the mixture starts to simmer and begins to thicken. This will happen quickly. Immediately remove from the heat and pour the custard into a bowl. Remove the vanilla bean and cover the hot pastry cream with a piece of plastic wrap to prevent a skin from forming. Let cool to room temperature, then refrigerate until cold and firm.

Agave Nectar Whipped Cream

MAKES | 1 QUART ☀ GLUTEN-FREE

This new-fashioned whipped cream makes any dessert just a little bit better. This is a great topping for ice cream treats or for use as a cake frosting or filling. To frost a large cake, increase this recipe by half; to frost and fill a cake, double the recipe.

2 cups heavy cream
5 tablespoons light agave nectar
1 tablespoon vanilla extract
Pinch of sea salt

Place the cream, agave nectar, vanilla extract, and salt in a bowl and beat with an electric mixer until stiff peaks form, approximately 2 to 3 minutes. Store the whipped cream in the refrigerator for 2 to 3 days.

Orange Crème Filling

MAKES | 2 CUPS

☀ VEGAN ☀ GLUTEN-FREE

Here's a delectable custard-style filling that's low-fat and dairy-free. It's delicious piped into the center of a cupcake for a creamy citrus surprise.

12 ounces firm silken tofu
⅓ cup plus 1 tablespoon light agave nectar
4 tablespoons nonhydrogenated
   butter substitute, melted
Pinch of sea salt
1½ teaspoons vanilla extract
½ teaspoon orange extract
1 tablespoon orange liqueur, such as
   Grand Marnier (optional)

In a food processor, blend the tofu with the agave nectar until very smooth and creamy, scraping down the sides of the bowl often. This will take several minutes. Add the butter substitute, salt, vanilla extract, orange extract, and orange liqueur if using. Blend well until completely smooth. Refrigerate to thicken. Store in the refrigerator for up to 5 days.

Chocolate Tofu Crème

MAKES | 2 CUPS

۞ VEGAN   ۞ GLUTEN-FREE

This vegan chocolate crème is a luxurious filling or topping for any cake. It produces a great custardlike quality thanks to the silken tofu. Add 1 or 2 tablespoons of your favorite liqueur to flavor this versatile filling. Try Amaretto, Frangelico, or Grand Marnier, for a special treat.

4 ounces unsweetened chocolate,
    chopped
12 ounces firm silken tofu
¾ cup light agave nectar
⅓ cup canola oil
1 tablespoon vanilla extract
Pinch of sea salt

Melt the chocolate in the microwave for 1½ to 2 minutes. In a food processor, blend the tofu and agave nectar until very smooth, about 2 to 3 minutes. Add the canola oil, melted chocolate, vanilla extract, and salt. Process until very smooth and creamy, scraping down the sides of the bowl occasionally, approximately 2 to 3 minutes. Store in the refrigerator for up to 2 weeks.

Lemon Tofu Crème

MAKES | 2 CUPS

۞ VEGAN   ۞ GLUTEN-FREE

This is a wonderful all-purpose topping for cakes, fresh fruit, granola, and more. Though the taste is rich and velvety, it's actually low fat and packed with protein as an added bonus.

12 ounces firm silken tofu
¼ cup light agave nectar
2½ tablespoons fresh lemon juice
2 tablespoons canola oil
1 teaspoon vanilla extract
⅛ teaspoon almond extract
Pinch of sea salt

Place the tofu, agave nectar, lemon juice, canola oil, vanilla extract, almond extract, and salt in a food processor. Blend well, scraping down the bowl until the mixture is very smooth, about 2 to 3 minutes. Chill before serving. Store in the refrigerator for up to 5 days.

Sweet Cherry Filling

MAKES | 1½ CUPS

❋ VEGAN   ❋ GLUTEN-FREE

Sweet cherries are delicious as a cake filling and make a luscious topping for cheesecake.

1 (10-ounce) bag frozen organic
   sweet cherries
½ cup water
⅓ cup light agave nectar
1½ tablespoons arrowroot powder
   dissolved in 1 tablespoon cold water
2 teaspoons lemon juice

Defrost the cherries and cut each one in half, checking for pits. Place the cherries, water, and agave nectar into a small saucepan. Bring to a boil and decrease the heat to a simmer. Cook for 3 to 4 minutes. Pour the arrowroot powder slurry into the simmering cherries. It should immediately thicken. Stir well, remove from the heat, and stir in the lemon juice. Chill thoroughly before using. Store in the refrigerator for up to 5 days.

Pineapple Cake Filling

MAKES | 1 QUART

❋ VEGAN   ❋ GLUTEN-FREE

This filling adds a little tropical flavor to a basic vanilla sponge cake. Frost it with whipped cream and you're done. For a special vegan dessert, top the Dairy-Free Cheesecake (page 62) with this sweet and tangy topping.

1 (20-ounce) can unsweetened crushed
   pineapple packed in its own juice
¾ cup water
3 tablespoons light agave nectar
1 tablespoon arrowroot powder dissolved
   in 2 tablespoons cold water

Bring the pineapple (including the juice), the water, and agave nectar to a boil in a small saucepan. Stir in the arrowroot powder slurry. Stir and cook until the mixture starts to thicken (this happens quickly). Cool to room temperature, then refrigerate before filling the cake. Store for up to 1 week in the refrigerator.

Hot Buttered Rum Sauce

MAKES | 1½ CUPS

This is a delectable and buttery-tasting sauce, guaranteed to take any dessert from simple to sublime in a single spoonful. You'll find one hundred and one reasons to add this to your favorite desserts.

½ cup amber agave nectar
½ cup heavy cream
½ cup evaporated skim milk
1 tablespoon arrowroot powder
   dissolved in 2 tablespoons water
2 tablespoons dark rum
1 teaspoon vanilla extract
2 teaspoons unsalted butter
Pinch of sea salt

Place agave nectar, cream, and milk in a saucepan on medium heat. Bring to a boil and decrease the heat to a simmer. Pour the arrowroot powder slurry into the saucepan and whisk until the mixture begins to thicken. Remove from the heat and whisk in the rum, vanilla extract, butter, and salt. Cool and store in the refrigerator for up to 2 weeks.

Raspberry Sauce

MAKES | 1½ CUPS

❀ VEGAN   ❀ GLUTEN-FREE

A refreshing and versatile sauce, this pairs nicely with ice cream, cake, fruit, and chocolate desserts. Make a couple of batches and divide into several small freezer storage bags and store frozen for up to 6 months.

1½ cups fresh raspberries, or
   1 (12-ounce) bag frozen unsweetened
   raspberries, defrosted
¼ to ⅓ cup light agave nectar
1 teaspoon arrowroot powder dissolved
   in 1 tablespoon cold water
½ teaspoon vanilla extract

Mash the raspberries through a sieve and discard the seeds. Place the raspberry purée and agave nectar in a small saucepan. Heat until almost boiling.

Taste the raspberries for sweetness, adding more agave nectar if necessary. Stir the arrowroot powder slurry into the raspberries and cook, stirring constantly, until the mixture starts to thicken (this happens quickly). Remove from the heat and stir in the vanilla extract. Cool before serving. Store in the refrigerator for up to 5 days, or in the freezer for several months.

Glossary of Ingredients

Agar

Agar is a sea vegetable gel primarily sold in flake or powder form. It has a jelling effect similar to gelatin. The best quality agar comes from Japan. Eden Foods and Mitoku brands are both readily available at most health food stores. Agar dissolves when boiled for several minutes in a liquid, unlike gelatin, which is not meant to be boiled. Agar will set quickly when refrigerated for about 1 hour.

Agave Nectar

Agave nectar is a delicious, low-glycemic liquid sweetener, made from the juice of the agave plant. It comes in light, amber, and raw varieties. See more on agave nectar in the introduction.

Arrowroot Powder

Arrowroot powder is a more digestible thickening agent than cornstarch and is used for sauces, puddings, and custards. It is also used in baking to create a finer texture. It comes from the dried powdered root of the arrowroot tuber. Mix it with a small amount of cold liquid to form a slurry before adding to dishes that require thickening. It requires less cooking than cornstarch. As soon as the mixture thickens, stop the cooking and remove from the heat. Overcooking arrowroot powder actually thins out a mixture.

Butter and Butter Substitutes

I use only unsalted butter in any recipe calling for butter, so I can control the exact amount of salt in a recipe. It has a much shorter shelf life than salted butter; therefore, I always store mine in the freezer, unless I know I'll be using it quickly.

The flavor of butter is hard to substitute in some desserts. However, I've tried to cut the amount used in recipes to a minimum.

For a dairy-free, vegan alternative to butter, I've found Earth Balance Natural Buttery Sticks vegetable oil spread to be a great choice. It's nonhydrogenated with no trans-fatty acids. It's made from non-GMO (genetically modified organism) expeller-pressed oils and can be equivalently substituted for butter in any recipe. Natural Buttery Sticks do contain some salt, so if you use them you should cut back on additional salt in a recipe.

Carob

Also known as St. John's bread and locust bean, the carob pod contains a sweet pulp that is dried and roasted, then ground to a powder. Unsweetened carob powder naturally has a slightly sweet taste. It is often used as a chocolate substitute, although most will agree that the taste is completely different.

Carob should not be perceived universally as a healthier alternative to chocolate. While the unsweetened powder used in baking is a sound nutritional choice, some carob chips and carob products contain more saturated fat and sugar than good quality chocolate. Carob can be a great substitute for individuals who are allergic to chocolate or cocoa powder and know that the taste will be uniquely delicious, but not identical to chocolate.

SunSpire makes an unsweetened carob chip that is still somewhat naturally sweet, and Chatfields makes a malt-sweetened carob chip that is a bit sweeter still. Both brands are available at most health food stores.

Chocolate and Cocoa

Since this is a cookbook on sugar-free cooking with agave nectar, the chocolate I use in all the included recipes is unsweetened. Here is where the quality of the chocolate is essential to a great finished product. Fine quality, unsweetened chocolate is not as readily available as its more popular counterparts—dark, bittersweet, semisweet, and so forth. Specialty and health food stores usually carry a limited offering of unsweetened chocolate. Internet sources are great for finding varieties of unsweetened chocolate. Let personal taste guide you to finding the chocolate you love best. I've experimented with several varieties, and my personal favorite is Valrhona's Cacao Pâte Extra, which is 100 percent percent cocoa. Since there is nothing added, this particular product is dairy-free and vegan. Those with gluten sensitivities should carefully check that the chocolate they choose meets their dietary requirements. Dagoba Organic Chocolate's Prima Materia is also outstanding, perfect for those who prefer a note of bitterness in their chocolate. Chocosphere, an Internet-only chocolate retailer, offers the finest quality chocolates from around the world. Short on time? Baker's Unsweetened Baking Chocolate, available in most supermarkets, will produce excellent results. Many of the high-quality unsweetened chocolate brands are sold in 2-pound blocks, so a small food scale is necessary for measuring accurately. Store chocolate in airtight, ziplock freezer bags in a dark, cool place.

Quality is also key when selecting unsweetened cocoa powder. My hands-down favorite is Green & Black's Organic Unsweetened Cocoa Powder. It's deep and dark, and the aroma and taste are rich and smooth. I would encourage you to try different brands to find your personal favorite. Chocolate is like wine: its taste depends on the source and variety of the cocoa beans used. It's definitely a matter of personal preference.

A few of my recipes call for chocolate chips. As of yet, there is no company marketing an agave nectar–sweetened chocolate chip, so I use a lower sugar, grain-sweetened chocolate chip from SunSpire.

Eggs

Eggs have taken a beating (no pun intended) in past years for being a major contributor to high cholesterol. Recent research has found, however, that dietary cholesterol is not the primary reason for high cholesterol levels in the blood. Instead, hereditary factors and an unbalanced diet with insufficient fiber, fresh fruit, and vegetables have more significant impact in most cases, according to experts.

Eating an occasional dessert with whole eggs is not likely to have a significant impact on cholesterol. However, I have used egg whites and egg substitutes (such as Egg Beaters) in recipes where the taste and texture would not be compromised. Eliminating the egg yolks does cut back somewhat on the fat in a recipe, which is helpful for those counting calories.

Recipes calling for whole eggs refer to the large size. For further health benefits, choose organic, cage-free, antibiotic-free eggs whenever possible. They are now widely available at any supermarket, as well as your local health food store.

Flavorings and Spices

To achieve the best results, it's essential to use the freshest spices and natural flavorings available. Buy vanilla beans fresh and keep them sealed in a jar for short-term use or frozen in freezer bags for extended storage. The flavor extracts I use are mainly organic, from a company called Frontier. They are sold at most natural food markets. Flavorganics is another organic extract company that makes a wide variety of extract flavors. If you are gluten-sensitive, make sure to buy extracts that are gluten-free (some ingredients or additives may contain gluten).

Flaxseeds

Also known as linseeds, flaxseeds are a rich source of alpha linolenic acid, an omega-3 fat that helps lower cholesterol and protect against heart disease. With their high soluble and nonsoluble fiber content, flaxseeds provide a nutritional boost to many muffin and cookie recipes.

Flaxseeds are best ground into a fine meal before using to aid the digestion and assimilation of their oils. They can also be left whole, if you are primarily looking to add fiber and texture to breads, muffins, and cookies.

I like to grind my own in a coffee grinder that has never been used for coffee (otherwise they will taste like coffee). Grind small amounts of flaxseeds and store in the refrigerator for no more than 2 to 3 days for maximum freshness. Sprinkle flaxseeds on cereals, yogurt, and fresh fruit for added fiber rich in omega-3s.

Flours

Whole grain flours—great sources for complex carbohydrates, fiber, B vitamins, minerals, and essential fatty acids—are necessary for creating delicious and nutritious desserts.

Sprouted Flours

I've used sprouted grain flours in most recipes due to their digestability and high nutrient content. When whole grains are sprouted, the starch molecules transform into vegetable sugars that are very easy to digest. In sprouted grains, nutrient levels increase and enzymes are created that aid digestion.

Creating sprouted grain flour is a multistep process. First grains are rinsed and soaked in hydrogen peroxide, then they are sprouted with warm water. Once the grains are sprouted, they are rinsed again at a high temperature to kill any surface bacteria that may have developed during the sprouting process. The grain is then dried in a dehydrator at 110°F after which time it is ready to be ground into flour.

I've used **sprouted spelt flour** in many of my recipes because of its light taste and texture. Spelt is low-gluten, but not gluten-free. I find spelt to be a very digestible grain, so I prefer it to wheat flour, though sprouted wheat flour can be used in most recipes as well.

Sprouted wheat flour is high in gluten and ground from red winter wheat. It has a nutty taste.

Find more information on organic sprouted flours and grains at the Summers Flour Co. website, www.creatingheaven.net.

Other Flours

Whole wheat pastry flour is milled from a lighter, softer whole wheat berry that has less gluten. It produces a light, delicate pastry and a tender cake texture.

Brown rice flour is a gluten-free product that creates a spongier texture in cakes and muffins. Its light color, taste, and texture makes it an ideal choice for crisp cookie recipes. It can be used in combination with other flours to make light, flaky piecrusts and crisp toppings.

Quinoa was the staple grain of the Inca civilization over five thousand years ago. Today quinoa is grown domestically in Colorado. It is a complete protein and works well as a gluten-free alternative to wheat in many recipes. It does, however, have a robust flavor that can compete with other ingredients in a recipe. The best uses for **quinoa flour** are in combination with other full-bodied flavors such as chocolate or carob, spices like cinnamon, and certain vegetables or fruits, like pumpkin or bananas. Experimentation is key to finding what appeals to your taste. It definitely should be included in everyone's diet for its powerhouse nutrients.

Milled from the root of the cassava plant, **tapioca flour** is essentially flavorless. Its fine texture works well in combination with other flours to produce delicious gluten-free baked goods. Also known as tapioca starch, it can be used as a thickening agent in soups, sauces, and puddings. Tapioca comes in many forms—flour, flake, and pearls.

Potato starch is derived from raw potatoes. It's an excellent thickener and widely used as an ingredient in gluten-free baking as it produces a tender, moist crumb. Added to other flours, potato starch creates a moist, soft texture in breads, rolls, and muffins.

Made from ground garbanzo beans, otherwise known as chickpeas, **garbanzo bean flour** is commonly used in Middle Eastern and European cooking. Garbanzo bean flour can be substituted for wheat on a $7/8$:1 ratio but works best when combined with other flours. In gluten-free whole grain baking, this flour produces cakes with a wonderful golden color and a delicate flavor. Plus it adds lots of healthy fiber and protein to many recipes.

Blanched almonds are finely ground to produce **almond meal** (also called almond flour). Rich and buttery flavored, almond meal has been widely used in Europe for making delicate cakes, pastries, and dessert fillings. Store almond meal in the refrigerator to retain its freshness.

Grain Beverages/Coffee Substitutes

I like to use caffeine-free instant powdered coffee substitutes in baking to intensify chocolate flavors or to produce mild coffee or mocha flavors in sauces or fillings. The best for baking is Pero Instant Natural Beverage, made from barley, chicory, and rye. It's a fine powder that dissolves easily in recipes. For a truer, stronger coffee flavor, Cafix or Kaffree Roma instant beverages are great. All are available at most natural food stores.

Guar Gum

A thickening agent and stabilizer, guar gum is derived from guar beans and generally sold in powder form. It's widely used in gluten-free baking to thicken dough to a proper consistency for leavening.

Milk, Soymilk, and Yogurt

I try to use mainly low-fat or nonfat dairy products as substitutes for the full-fat variety whenever possible. One such versatile product is a **nonfat Greek-style plain yogurt** that I use often. This yogurt is strained, so its texture is thick and rich, with no fat. Due to its active cultures, yogurt is more digestible than milk. I often dilute it with water in recipes calling for buttermilk, regular yogurt, sour cream, or crème fraîche. It keeps baked goods moist and also makes a creamy and delicious frozen yogurt.

Until recently, strained yogurt was hard to find, but now most major supermarkets and health food stores carry FAGE brand and Trader Joe's also sells a great product marketed under their own label. Read the labels carefully for the 0 percent fat variety, as the whole milk variety contains 20 grams of fat in 7 ounces.

For a milk alternative, **unsweetened soy milk** has been my choice in many recipes. Most other milk alternatives such as rice, hemp, nut milks, and most soy milks contain some form of sweetener. Blue Diamond brand is now producing an unsweetened line of low-fat, low-calorie almond milks (regular, vanilla, and chocolate). I found these didn't work so well in my recipes but they are great for drinking.

Not to be confused with soy flour, **instant soy milk powder** is made from cooked soybeans that have been finely ground. It can be mixed with water to make soy milk or as a baking additive. It has a distinctive nutty flavor, so taste and experiment before adding to recipes with very delicate flavors.

Made from fresh skimmed milk that is dried to powder form, **nonfat dry milk** can be reconstituted with water to make skim milk. The powder also can be used in sauces, ice creams, and desserts to thicken and enrich the flavors and textures of the products. One brand I particularly like is Organic Valley's Organic Non-Fat Dry Milk, which is produced without hormones or antibiotics. It can be found at most health food stores.

Nonstick Cooking Oil Spray

I use canola oil cooking spray for greasing pans to ensure easy, stick-free release of cakes and other baked goods. You won't need much to do the trick; a light spray is all that's required. Avoid spraying too much on the sides of the pans because cakes need a nonslippery surface to rise best.

Nuts

Buy raw nuts to use in baking. Roasted nuts can turn rancid quickly if not refrigerated due to the breakdown of their oils that have been heated. If a recipe calls for toasted nuts, bake the raw nuts for 10 to 12 minutes at 350°F just prior to using. Let the nuts cool before proceeding with the recipe. To maintain their freshness, store toasted nuts in the refrigerator.

Oils

For me, the oil that works best in baking is neutral-flavored, unrefined, organic expeller-pressed **canola oil**. This kind of canola oil is not mass-produced and has not been exposed to chemicals in its processing. A natural food market is the best source for quality oils.

Coconut oil has been in the news recently for its health benefits, a complete turnaround from the past. Although it contains saturated fat, it comes from a plant source, and the body metabolizes very differently from animal fats. Made up of medium-chain fatty acids, coconut oil contains no cholesterol and may in fact aid in increasing metabolism and promoting weight loss. Unrefined, extra-virgin coconut oil contains the most beneficial nutrients, but it also imparts a strong coconut taste. The refined variety eliminates the coconut flavor. Only you can decide if the coconut taste will be acceptable in a recipe. I've used both, depending on the complementary flavors. You'll find coconut oil in health food stores and many Internet shopping sites.

Sea Salt

All my recipes using salt call for sea salt. I'd like to specify further that I use Celtic Sea Salt exclusively in my cooking and baking. Celtic Sea Salt comes from the pristine salt marshes of Brittany in France. It comes in many varieties: light gray coarse for salt grinders, light gray fine-ground salt, and Flower of the Ocean (or fleur de sel), a delicate flavored salt. The light gray variety is best used for cooking and baking, while the precious Flower of the Ocean is wonderful sprinkled on salads or other foods as a finishing salt. These delicious salts are highly nutritious and are harvested by hand, never bleached or treated with chemicals. The salt supplies more than eighty vital minerals essential to good health. Laboratory analyses are done annually to maintain the highest standards.

Tofu

Tofu is a mild-tasting bean curd made from soy milk. It is high in protein, low in calories, cholesterol-free, and contains no saturated fat. High in nutrients called isoflavones, tofu has been shown by scientific findings to help protect against illnesses such as heart disease, cancer, and osteoporosis.

Tofu is available in a variety of firmnesses and textures. The best tofu for use in desserts is the silken variety. Mori-Nu makes a silken tofu that comes in 12.3-ounce aseptic packages that require no refrigeration until opened. It comes in regular and light varieties; the latter reduces the calories and fat per serving slightly. I recommend the regular firm variety for use in recipes for fillings and toppings because of its taste and texture. The light tofu is added to cakes and baked goods without a noticeable difference in the end product.

Tofu is one of the most versatile ingredients available for desserts. It acts as a binder in baked goods. One quarter cup (2 ounces) of tofu has the same protein and moisture content as one large egg. Tofu can also be used to make great creamy sauces, toppings, and fillings for cakes and pies. Even if you don't like tofu, I encourage you to give it a try in a dessert recipe.

Xanthan Gum

A thickening agent and stabilizer, Xanthan gum comes from the pure culture fermentation of the microorganism *Xanthomonas campestris*. During processing, its coating is removed, dried, and milled into a powder. It is commonly used as a substitute for gluten in baked goods.

Sources

THE FOLLOWING LIST OF SOURCES SHOULD HELP YOU LOCATE many of the specialized ingredients used in this book, as well as other high-quality products that will help you create a well-stocked natural food pantry. Remember, your local natural food market is the best place to shop for most items. As a general rule, the staff is very familiar with the products, willing to answer questions, and can special-order items they may not carry on a regular basis.

Agave Nectar Sources

Essential Living Foods
12304 Santa Monica Boulevard
#218
Los Angeles, CA 90025
(310) 571-3272
www.essentiallivingfoods.com
Organic premium and raw agave nectars

Madhava Honey Co.
Highway 66
Lyons, CO 80540
(303) 823-5166
www.madhavahoney.com
*Organic light and amber wild
agave nectar*

Nekutli Agave Nectar
(The Colibree Company, Inc.)
P.O. Box 1549
Aspen, CO 81612
(866) 635-8854
www.agavenectar.com
*Organic light, amber, and dark
agave nectars*

Ohgave! Agave Nectars
300 Center Drive, Suite G
Superior, CO 80027
(303) 588-4107
www.ohgave.com
*Premium, 100% Blue Weber agave nectars in
light, amber, raw, natural maple, and honey flavor
varieties. Agave nectar sweetened products*

Sweet Cactus Farms
10317 Washington Boulevard
Los Angeles, CA 90232
(310) 733-4343
www.sweetcactusfarms.com
*Organic light and dark blue
agave nectars*

Wholesome Sweeteners
8016 Highway 90-A
Sugar Land, TX 77478
(800) 680-1896
www.wholesomesweeteners.com
*Organic light, amber, and raw
blue agave nectars*

Other Products

After the Fall Products, Inc.
1700 Clark Road
Havre de Grace, MD 21078
(800) 544-9857
www.atfjuices.com
Organic fruit juices

Arrowhead Mills, Inc.
Box 2059
Hereford, TX 79045
(800) 749-0730
www.arrowheadmills.com
High-quality flours, baking ingredients, and cereals

Berlin Natural Bakery
P.O. Box 311
Berlin, OH 44610
(800) 686-5334
www.berlinnaturalbakery.com
Sprouted spelt bread, whole grain spelt breads

Bob's Red Mill Natural Foods
5209 S.E. International Way
Milwaukee, OR 97222
(800) 553-2258
www.bobsredmill.com
Flaxseeds, flax meal, whole grain organic flours, almond and hazelnut flours, and baking products

The Bridge Tofu
598 Washington Street
Middletown, CT 06457
(860) 346-3663
www.bridgetofu.com
Tofu, amasake, seitan

Cascadian Farm (General Mills)
P.O. Box 9452
Minneapolis, MN 55440
(800) 624-4123
www.cascadianfarm.com
Frozen organic fruit and vegetables, fruit spreads, and cereals

Ceres Fruit Juices (PFY) Ltd.
(Imported by Stanmar International, Inc.)
Bon Chrétien Street
Ceres, South Africa 6835
(800) 905-1116
www.ceresjuices.com
100 percent natural, no preservatives, no sugar added fruit juices

Chatfield's (Liberty Richter)
300 Broadacres Drive
Bloomfield, NJ 07003
(973) 338-0300
www.libertyrichter.com
Unsweetened carob chips, unsweetened carob, and cocoa powders

Chocosphere, LLC
P.O. Box 2237
Tualatin, OR 97062
(877) 992-4626
www.chocosphere.com
Internet-only shop offering high-quality chocolate from around the world

Earth Balance (owned and distributed by GFA Brands, Inc.)
P.O. Box 397
Cresskill, NJ 07626
(201) 568-9300
www.earthbalance.net
Nonhydrogenated, trans-fat and dairy-free butter substitutes

Eden Foods, Inc.
701 Tecumseh Road
Clinton, MI 49236
(800) 248-0320
www.edenfoods.com
Organic soy and rice milks, agar flakes,
mirin, organic imports from Japan

Erewhon (U.S. Mills)
200 Reservoir Street
Needham, MA 02494
(800) 422-1125
www.usmillsinc.com
Organic, low-sugar, low-salt crisp brown rice
cereals and other whole grain cereals

Essential Eating Sprouted Foods
P.O. Box 771
Waverly, PA 18471
(570) 586-1557
www.essentialeating.com
Sprouted spelt and wheat flours

FAGE USA
25-26 50th Street
Woodside, NY 11377
(718) 204-5323
www.fageusa.com
Greek-style strained yogurt

Flavorganics
268 Doremus Avenue
Newark, NJ 07105
(888) 674-3528
www.flavorganics.com
Organic, pure-flavored extracts

Frontier Natural Products Co-op
P.O. Box 299
3021 78th Street
Norway, IA 52318
(800) 669-3275
www.frontiercoop.com
All natural and organic extracts,
U.S.-produced spices

Green & Black's USA, Inc.
389 Interspace Parkway
Parsippany, NJ 07054
(877) 299-1254
www.greenandblacks.com
Organic, unsweetened cocoa powder

Jay Robb Enterprises, Inc.
6339 Paseo del Lago
Carlsbad, CA 92008
(877) JAY-ROBB
www.jayrobb.com
Sugar-free protein powder supplements

Lakewood Juices
P.O. Box 420708
Miami, FL 33242-0708
(305) 324-5900
www.lakewoodjuices.com
100 percent pure fruit juices

Mori-Nu (Morinaga
Nutritional Foods, Inc.)
2441 West 205th Street,
Suite C102
Torrance, CA 90501
(310) 787-0200
www.morinu.com
Silken tofu, all varieties including organic

Next Proteins (America's Whey Protein Co.)
P.O. Box 2469
Carlsbad, CA 92018
(800) DESIGNER
www.designerwhey.com
Sugar-free protein powder supplements

Now Foods
395 South Glen Ellyn Road
Bloomingdale, IL 60108
(888) 669-3663
www.nowfoods.com
Xanthum and guar gums, whole grain flours,
soy milk powder, flaxseeds and meal, and
natural food products and supplements

Quinoa Corporation
P.O. Box 279
Gardena, CA 90248
(310) 217-8125
www.quinoa.net
All quinoa products: quinoa grain, flour, and pasta

Silk Soymilks (White Wave Foods Co.)
12002 Airport Way
Broomfield, CO 80021
(888) 820-9283
www.silksoymilk.com
Organic unsweetened soy milk, organic
soy creamer

Soyatoo
(Imported by Ceres Organics)
2121 30th Street
Boulder, CO 80301
(866) 542-1559
www.ceresorganics.com
www.soyatoo-usa.com
Whipped soy topping

Spectrum Organic Products, LLC
(Hain Celestial Group)
5341 Old Redwood Highway,
Suite 400
Petaluma, CA 94954
(800) 998-2705
www.spectrumorganics.com
Organic oils, refined and unrefined coconut oils

SunSpire Natural Foods
(SunSpired Natural Foods, Inc.)
1850 Fairway Drive
San Leandro, CA 94577
(510) 346-3860
www.sunspire.com
Grain-sweetened chocolate and carob chips

Trader Joe's
stores nationwide
(800) 746-7857
www.traderjoes.com
Natural and organic products,
Greek-style yogurt, frozen organic fruit

Westsoy
(Hain Celestial Group, Inc.)
58 South Service Road
Melville, NY 11747
(800) SOY-MILK
www.westsoy.biz
Organic, unsweetened plain, vanilla,
and chocolate soy milks

Index